Buying a California Business

The Ultimate Guide for Savvy Business Buyers!

Peter Siegel, MBA

Peter Siegel, MBA
Buying A California Business

Printed in the United States of America

ISBN: 0-9761985-1-7

Library Of Congress Control Number: 2004113204

Bulk Quantity Discounts:
This book and companion books from this publisher are available at quantity discounts for bulk purchases for educational, business or sales promotional use. For information regarding bulk purchases please call (800) 572-7260.

Publisher:
California Businesses For Sale / www.bizben.com
9110-B Alcosta Blvd., #238
San Ramon, CA. 94583
(800) 572-7260

Other books by Peter Siegel, MBA, available from this publisher:
Selling a California Business -
   The Ultimate Guide for California Business Sellers!
Businesses For Sale -
   A Guide for Business Buyers, Business Owners & Business Brokers

See our website at: www.bizben.com

Featuring the Successful bizben Method!

ACKNOWLEDGEMENTS

For the past 15 years, it has been my privilege to be associated with a number of creative, dedicated and talented people in my work as a business buyer, business seller, business broker and founder and president of a growing organization that facilitates the marketing of small businesses for sale throughout California.

I am indebted to a number of professionals, too numerous to mention, from whom I have gained the education and the inspiration, as well as the ideas and the insights which I endeavor to share with others on the pages of this book.

I am grateful for the opportunities I have had to learn and to grow in this fascinating and vital area of business.

Peter Siegel, MBA
January, 2005

*Small businesses are a key component of the California Economy; and one of the best
ways to increase affluence or enjoy riches.*

INTRODUCTION

If you are considering joining the ranks of California's small business owners, you will become a member of a fairly exclusive club – there are roughly one million of us able to generate enough revenues, either in our one or two-person businesses or with employees, to provide a living for ourselves and our families. If that seems like a large number of entrepreneurs, remember that there are nearly 35 million Californians so we sill make up a rather unique segment of society.

Owners of small (with values under $5 million) businesses in California contribute significantly to our economy, providing jobs for millions of people, pouring millions of dollars into the state's coffers through the taxes we pay, and millions more to the Federal government. We are professionals, builders, dealers, proprietors, shop owners, service technicians, sales executives, consultants, trainers, engineers, experts in a number of fields. We are the embodiment of the American Dream, working to improve our communities, setting examples for others to follow.

I commend you for your courage and your vision – important qualities of today's entrepreneur.

And I hope you will find, within these pages, a bit of inspiration and plenty of practical ideas that will help to make your dream of business ownership a reality.

Good luck in your venture.

CHAPTER ONE

WHAT IT TAKES TO BE A SUCCESSFUL BUSINESS OWNER

Every day, scores of Californians launch a start up company or buy an existing business, and join the growing ranks of people, from every part of the state, who own a small business – that is, an operation with a value under $5 million; most of them worth less than $1 million.

Among these people may be a future multi-millionaire or a budding civic and political leader. Many of these entrepreneurs will – through their ideas, their skills and their labor – provide jobs and tax revenues for local communities, as well as products and services that may benefit people throughout the global economic community.

The courage they demonstrate by striking out on their own, in either a new or existing business, serves as a testament to the American sense of self-sufficiency and the spirited California attitude.

Some may have had a little "encouragement" – a lost job, for example, providing the impetus to determine it's time to become self employed. Others simply see the writing on the economic wall and recognize that the secure wage-earner positions with benevolent companies that employed our parents are truly a relic of the past. "If I want a bright career future," is the current reasoning, "I'll have to create it for myself."

It must be noted, of course that the majority of these freshly-minted enterprises won't make it to their fourth birthdays. And seven years out from start, there are, perhaps only ten percent of these companies still in existence. And along with these casualties, of course, are long-established companies that, for one reason or another, reach the end of their lives.

Not Everyone is Cut Out to Be a Capable Business Owner

Why don't most businesses survive? For anyone curious about this, there is a treasure trove of information – hundreds of books in libraries and book stores, thousands of pages on the Internet and truck loads of studies and reports available from governmental agencies and private research organizations – all providing answers. They point to a number of factors including insufficient financing, poor timing, lack of planning, unreceptive market, failure to execute effectively, anemic economic conditions, inadequately conceived ideas, health problems of principals and overwhelming competitive forces.

I think the number one factor is simply that the would-be entrepreneur liked the idea of being in business for himself or herself, but doesn't have what it takes to be successful in this endeavor. Just because someone has a dream of owning their own enterprise, calling the shots, enjoying the riches and privileges they think come with business ownership, doesn't mean they have what it takes to make it work.

Management Ability-Not Necessarily Inherited

A Southern California printing company started just after WWII was a family business with the third generation assuming management in the early 1990s. And the founder's grandson seemed to have everything working for his success. He had earned a business degree while working part time at the firm in nearly every capacity – janitor, press operator, route drive, office assistant, shipping clerk, marketing intern – so he was very familiar with every operation. Besides, he had a passion for the business, and had been picturing himself at its manager, ever since he started helping out at the plant in his early teens.

Under his management everything appeared to be running smoothly – at least at first. But by the third year it was obvious that the dramatic shift in the industry, brought on by the desktop publishing revolution, was beginning to impact the company in a negative way. Nothing had prepared the young owner/operator to recognize and adapt to the dramatic changes in the business. And he lacked the instincts and leadership qualities that were needed to navigate the company over the industry's challenging new landscape. Rather than face reality and take action, he convinced himself the digital workflow being adopted by customers and competitors was a passing trend; that things would soon return to the way they'd been in the past.

In 2000 the printing company closed its doors and the most recent owner – the third generation of its management – found himself out of work with no prospects and nothing to brag about on his resume. People who knew him thought he'd done a good job as a printing press operator – the part time job he'd held with the company during his last year in college. But he was clearly not equipped to run a business. Even though his grandfather and his father had the talents and aptitudes required to lead the company's expansion for five decades, those characteristics had not been passed on to their progeny.

Characteristics Needed for Success

So, what are the characteristics that account for success as a business owner?

Once again, the theories are endless. A search of the literature reveals that analysts and consultants from various industries, as well as business educators and human resources professionals all have their favorite ideas about what personal traits and working habits lead to success for business owners. Some stress the importance of having a take charge personality while others feel it's more critical to be able to work with others in a collaborative way. Are leaders always firm in carrying through on their decisions or is it better to be flexible so as to change tactics with evolving circumstances?

And while there is no absolute unanimity about what qualities always insure success, there are eight themes that continue to pop up among the favorite characteristics cited by those who study the world of business to learn what leads to winning, and to losing. They are:

The proactive personality

Those who become too impatient waiting for the permission that is supposed to approve their actions – simply moving forward without it – exhibit characteristics of the proactive personality. This impulse to act while others are in discussion is widely recognized as an important quality among leaders, although it's not a particularly popular trait for a good corporate citizen. In settings where the working style embraces team building and consensus decisions, people with a proactive way of conducting business have a difficult time. They may struggle to make headway with their ideas and ambitions, floundering in corporate management, usually somewhere in the middle rung. They can advance part of the way up the ladder due to their energy and aggressiveness, but they're often prevented from moving to the top of the organization because they annoy their superiors and confuse colleagues and subordinates who are used to the more orderly way of doing things.

In many cases, those in corporations who are proactive in their approach eventually strike out on their own, pulling together the resources they need to prove their ideas, getting the opportunity they want, to make it, or to fail on their own terms.

If your teachers, your bosses, and those with whom you've worked have described you as a self starter, or one who frequently takes initiative, you can consider this an indication you're seen as a proactive individual.

Without the modifying effects of other important characteristics, this tendency can do more damage than good. So it's not necessarily a desirable characteristic operating in a vacuum. But it is a necessary quality for those who want to be successful in their own enterprise.

Determination

A cousin to proactive behavior is the desire and, what's more, the drive to sustain the action. It is an essential trait for those who mean to strike out on their own – whether they're engaged in building an entirely new enterprise from scratch, or modestly offering a familiar product or service that fills an obvious niche, or some entrepreneurial activity in between. If you possess this quality, it means you will do what it takes to push past resistance and obstacles if you can, or find new avenues to use in reaching your goals if the current pathways are blocked.

From the fire of determination comes the energy to persist. And this quality is rarer than you might think. Yes, many people claim that they are determined to achieve their objectives, willing to be persistent in the labor needed to achieve their goals. Yet the majority of us abandon projects when we discover there's more work or difficulty involved than we'd anticipated. We give up trying to sell our ideas after we've been told "no" repeatedly. Or we're so distracted with family and other obligations, or by the constant barrage of media messages, that we find it impossible to maintain focus on the subject at hand. Instead of completing a planned activity, we offer the explanation that: "I meant to do it but I just didn't have the time (or money, or assistance)."

You've probably heard that a poor plan well executed is more productive than a good plan with inadequate follow through. Determination, of course is the difference. In the words of a 17th Century Cleric, Thomas Fuller: "(In) determination … lies the great distinction between great men and little men."

Ability to develop a vision

I consider these characteristics – the urge to take action, and the quality of determination so that action will be sustained – to comprise two of the four pillars which form the foundation of effective leadership. The third is the ability to formulate a clear idea of what the business should look like, so that the leader and everyone else in the organization has a common picture that serves to guide their efforts.

How many business people do you know who have plenty of enthusiasm for the work of their organization – who continue to create new opportunities and are able to sustain a high level of activity – but manage to push their companies around in circles, without a clear direction in which to move? I know too many people who fit this description – not only in business but also in government and the non-profit sector. And I've seen them enjoy success when times are good – customers are plentiful and things run fairly smoothly. But if management doesn't have a firm and clear idea of where the organization is going, I think the ultimate destination is disaster.

This is a common malady of small businesses in California. And it's not always obvious at first. An owner without a vision for the business may feel that it is enough of a management objective to simply build sales and profits.

But how does that person choose between short and long-term strategies? Is the marketing effort focused on service, low price, convenience or perceived value?

Should the owner develop and reward a few highly trained employees or is it better to get by with a succession of low-wage workers?

Ultimately, I don't think a proactive and determined leader will be successful at business without a clear direction in which to lead.

Some planning skill

The fourth pillar is the ability to plan – to develop a blue print which helps to channel the proactive behavior and to focus the determination in a way meant to realize the vision.

Some business owners are excellent planners, others need considerable help. I don't think a successful manager needs to be a brilliant strategist, or have the calculating ability of a chess champion. But it is important to be able to understand the current condition of your organization in relation to what you envision for it, and then be able to determine what steps are needed to move from today's position to the objective you want to achieve.

Many business experts regard the lack of planning to be the number one cause of failure among businesses. Certainly it is becoming an increasingly vital part of management. The environment in which we do business is changing at an accelerating rate because of the adoption of new technologies, the global character of the business landscape, and the way the media – including the Internet – influences our habits of collecting information, making buying decisions, conducting business and consuming goods and services. A manager who can't anticipate the future – at least in a broad outline – and then determine how to prepare his or her organization to function successfully in that scenario, soon will be presiding over a failing operation.

Skill and knowledge about the work of the enterprise

Most of us have a relatively clear idea about where our talents and interests lie. So it is not likely we would choose a business for which we have no emotional or intellectual appreciation. There are exceptions, of course, such as the selection of a business only for the reason that it looks like it generates a substantial profit. Or someone may choose an opportunity simply because it's affordable, compared to other companies which might be of more interest. If a business owner in such a situation does not attempt to learn and to become interested in the enterprise, he or she may well be headed for failure.

Whenever one of the clients whom I consult about buying a business tells me that a particular opportunity meets some of the criteria, but that "I just can't see myself going there every day," I advise that the client continue to look for something that will be more appealing.

Knowing how to balance the competing needs for firmness and flexibility

As a young employee in various jobs during my high school and college years, I attempted to be guided by the business principles I was learning, and felt they should be adhered to at all times. So, it would confuse me when I witnessed an owner or manager compromise with a customer whom I thought was in the wrong. And I didn't understand why my boss would ignore the inappropriate behavior of an employee. I thought the businesses would not survive if those in charge weren't willing to stand up for what was clearly the right principle, each and every time.

To make things even more confusing, I noticed that there were times when a boss ushered a demanding customer to the door with instructions not to come back. And I observed how some vendors could get away with sloppy bookkeeping and poor packaging up to a point, and then one day they'd be taken off the supplier list and we'd stop receiving their merchandise.

As I matured and began to learn more about how business really is conducted, I started to develop a sense about the balance between sticking strictly to the basic principles of business and loosening up the enforcement of the rules when suitable.

How do you know what is the correct way to handle these matters? While no manager is always perfect in achieving this balance, the ability to consistently act in the best long-term interests of the organization is an art, probably an art that is developed over a period of time. And it is an important quality for a successful small business owner.

Achieving the proper balance is important in a number of areas – not just in relating to customers, employees and vendors. The third generation printing company owner mentioned at the beginning of this chapter was firm in his beliefs about the way to conduct the business. Perhaps he should have been more flexible – more open to new ways of doing things, along the lines being adopted elsewhere in his industry.

And yet there were companies in the printing business, during the same period of time, that were so eager to be flexible – to adopt new tools and techniques – that they neglected some of their core values. They eagerly advocated a new proofing system, for example, that let customers view their materials on their own computer screens before it went to press. It seemed like a good idea because of the speed at which this operation could be conducted. And what convenience! No more time-consuming press checks. The problem with these early systems, however, is that printing quality and color consistency was sacrificed. Printers who failed to adhere to basics, with respect to the product quality concerns of their customers, went out of business as quickly – having been too flexible – as did the company with the too rigid management.

Good health and stamina

Get ready for the 12-hour day, perhaps lots of them, strung together over weeks or months of building your business, attending to customers and getting new ones.

The picture some people have of a business owner spending afternoons on the golf course with customer/friends is only partially accurate. What they don't tell you is that the person may have to go back to the office or the shop for another six or eight hours to catch up on work, before calling it a day. And you don't hear about the years of struggle, sacrifice and near starvation invested by the owner to achieve the point where a few hours can be enjoyed in a leisure activity.

In addition to the grueling hours, business owners are subjected to a lot of pressure that may not be experienced by their friends in the corporate world. Your decisions as head of your own operation can affect the future of the company, the future for your employees, not to mention your family's economic well-being. Can you deal with the responsibilities, and the pressure? Can you persist despite some sleepless nights and the occasional need to make a stomach-churning decision?

You will get out from under that obnoxious boss and the co workers you don't like. No job is perfect. But most business owners feel their work now makes more demands than ever – more pressures that they'd never experienced when on someone else's payroll.

Ability to function in the real business world

Those entering the world of small business ownership should keep your dreams in tact. Picturing your ideal business provides the motivation you'll need to withstand the aggravation and the sometimes unrelenting demands that will be placed on you. At the same time, it's absolutely necessary that you can accept and work with the hard realities that will appear in front of you, sometimes block the way, on the journey toward your dream.

There is no perfect business. Any would-be buyers who are holding out for a combination of low price and limited down payment, to get into an absolutely secure, highly profitable operation that is easy to manage part time and also fun to be involved with, had better get ready for a long, long, search. And you're not likely to find perfect employees, customers and vendors. Nor are you likely to do business with the world's most generous landlord or franchisor.

You'll discover, in the following pages that every business on the market will come with flaws or disadvantages. Perhaps you'll learn from this book how to spot imperfections in a small business that can be overcome, and you may get some insight that will help you to attack and fix these problems. But you won't learn where to find the perfect business because there are none. The ability to acknowledge and work with this and other facts of business life is an important quality for someone who wants to be a successful entrepreneur.

If you're considering the idea of purchasing a business, your first step ought to be a little self examination using these eight qualities as guidelines. How do you measure up?

Conclusion

Poor management is a prime cause of failure among young businesses as well as long-established ones. As a guide for the reader, eight characteristics of good management are reviewed so potential business owners can gain insight into what it takes to be successful.

KEY POINTS FROM THIS CHAPTER

❖ *Among the scores of new small business formations that occur in California every day – and even among existing companies – there are a number of failures resulting from various factors, chiefly incapable management.*

❖ *A 50+-year-old family-run printing company in Northern California went out of business because the grandson of the founder did not have what it takes to keep the company on track during dramatic changes in the industry. So much for the idea that leadership ability is "in the genes."*

❖ *Among eight characteristics considered to be needed for success as a business owner, is a proactive personality, also referred to as a self starter.*

❖ *Strong determination, coupled with a proactive approach, is one of the key qualities for a capable business owner to operate successfully.*

❖ *A vision for his or her company allows an owner to determine what goals to work toward.*

❖ *For a small California business to thrive, particularly in a challenging business environment, it is critical that the owner is able to create and implement effective planning.*

❖ *Although business buyers sometimes are interested mostly in the profitability of a business, a smart buyer will make sure he or she is familiar with the work of the purchased company and the basics of its industry.*

❖ *Having the talent to balance competing needs for firmness and flexibility as a manager is an important quality for a business owner.*

❖ *Because business ownership is usually a demanding responsibility, involving long hours and hard work, it's important that the head of a small California company enjoy good health and ample stamina.*

❖ *One critical quality for a successful small business owner is the ability to manage with realistic expectations.*

CHAPTER TWO

SOME CHOICES TO MAKE

If you have decided to purchase a small California business you have – whether or not you know it – set out for yourself a most demanding task. There is a great deal of work involved and countless decisions to make. And, as mentioned in the first chapter, this campaign could easily take a year or more to complete.

We tackled, as the place to start, the question of whether you really have what it takes to be a successful small business owner. If you've concluded that you are ready for the challenge, the next step – which we'll cover here – is to begin to focus your search by making some basic choices about the kind of business you want.

It also is important that you make some decisions about what you will bring to the business – how much money you will have available, what level of debt you're willing to assume and how many hours every week you expect to work at your new business. We'll touch on these matters in the next chapter.

Buying Rather Than Starting from Scratch

Incidentally, since you are reading this book about buying an existing company, it's likely that you have decided to take over an ongoing enterprise rather than to start one from scratch. What you'll find in these pages, of course, is some information, advice and ideas about buying a small California business from someone else, either the founder or a successive owner. If you are not yet sure about the best way for you to go – buy or startup – you'll want to find some assistance in the area of business startups to go along with this book so that you can make a more informed choice.

If your decision is to purchase an existing business you can look forward to the benefits of a built-in base of customers, an infrastructure of systems in place, a history of earnings, vendor relationships, the training and help of an outgoing owner, and possibly a more manageable investment structure – that offers some seller financing – compared to the requirement that you come up with all the cash needed to launch a company from the very start.

Those entering the world of entrepreneurship stand a better chance of success by their acquisition of a proven business than if they go into the marketplace with a startup. It is estimated that only one in ten new small California businesses will still be operating in seven years following inception. The survival rate for existing businesses which change hands is much higher.

Full or Part-Time Involvement

If your choice is to search among existing businesses for sale with the idea that there may be one just right for you, the next decision may concern the amount of involvement that is required to operate it.

Anyone researching business offerings in California has probably encountered those described as "absentee." The implication here – and it usually is encouraged by the seller or broker for such a business – is that the new owner will be able to enjoy the income and other benefits of business ownership without having to work.

I agree that the idea of an absentee business is quite appealing, but I should reveal that I have yet to come across a business offering that you merely wind up and let run by itself. The closest may be coin operated enterprises, such as a laundromat, a self-serve car wash, and some kinds of vending routes. These businesses can be manageable on a part-time basis because customers take care of themselves using your equipment. And you may be able to get a trusted employee to clear out the cash boxes, wipe down the machinery, replace product in vend slots and make sure that related operational matters are handled. I've known of partnerships that buy such businesses, each person putting in part of the purchase price then taking turns visiting the premises to sweep the floors and conduct the other maintenance functions.

If a part-time business is appealing, you should be aware that well run enterprises of this type are difficult to find on the market. And they frequently bring purchase prices at a higher multiple of earnings – on the order of four or more – than businesses that will demand more of your time. The idea of earnings multiples will be covered in more detail in the chapter that reviews business pricing.

What concerns many buyers investigating part-time businesses of this type is the difficulty of obtaining reliable information about revenues. I've seen sellers give their listener a wink or a little grin while they explain that the business deals only in cash, and so you can report whatever income you want. Perhaps that's good news for buyers whose objective is to hide their earnings from the taxing authorities. But it doesn't answer the question of how much return a buyer might expect for his or her investment.

Buyers are well advised to be skeptical, even when presented with a P&L for a part-time business that deals with cash. You won't find work orders, monthly customer statements, vendor invoices, receivables ledgers and other documentation that usually helps to verify the performance of most companies. The best approach I know of, when investigating say, a coin operated laundry, is to review the utility bills so you can determine the consumption of water, electricity and gas during any given period. Then contact the manufacturers of the equipment used in the business to learn about the water and power use ratings for the washers and driers. The next step is to do a little math so you can determine how many washes and dries were dispensed during the time period under study. Based on the vend prices, you should be able to calculate the income within a few dollars.

Beware, however, of owners who let their machines run when no one is observing them, or keep the wash basin spigots open so as to run up their water and utility bills and attempt to misrepresent the level of their customer activity. That is why, whenever I have worked with buyers interested in a business like this, I insist on three or more years of utility bills to examine and I look carefully to see if usage pattern have been consistent.

You may be a business buyer for whom part time involvement is exactly the right solution. You can continue in your job with your enterprise providing extra income and some tax benefits. And if you can build the company's profitability you can look forward to a gain when it is sold.

Most buyers of small California businesses, however, expect to be present in their company every day, all day, to take care of customers, handle orders and manage the other aspects that require their attention. And if they're not in the office or elsewhere in their facility they're calling on prospects, meeting with vendors or conducting other business related to the company.

To Be or Not To Be a Franchisee

The familiar choices among risk, independence and reward are at issue if you are considering becoming part of a franchised business system. The likelihood of your company remaining profitable is greater if it's a franchise than if it is a non-franchise opportunity. But this reduced risk comes at a cost of limitations in the way you operate and sometimes in the amount of money you can make. Here are some things to consider when contemplating whether to sign on with a franchise business or become the new owner of an independent company:

The brand

You don't have to own a branch of a world-renowned fast-food chain to enjoy the benefits of belonging to a franchise. There are hundreds of franchise organizations in food, personal and business services, and other industries that confer on their members a sizeable slice of the business in their markets because of a recognizable name and, by inference, a respected reputation. And if your franchisor has been promoting the brand – building visibility among likely customers – much of the marketing work in your area has been done. You may balk at the fees charged to franchisees for advertising but in most cases it's a good deal. You'll gain more visibility for your business by being included in these massive promotions than if you were to spend twice that amount trying to gain attention as an individual operator.

There is, of course, another side to this: An important component of a good brand is consistency in delivering the goods and services, so the customer experience is identical throughout the system. Whether someone visits an outlet in downtown Los Angeles or in a rural town in the Sierra Nevadas, he or she will find the appearance of the premises, the choices offered and the way the staff performs to be pretty much the same. To achieve this uniformity the franchisor establishes and enforces a full set of specifications covering everything from the look of its branches to the most mundane aspects of each employee's performance. Along with the keys to your franchise establishment on your first day you'll receive a book of rules that you'll be expected to study and perhaps memorize. And of course you'll be held accountable for the adherence to those rules by everyone whom you employ. If your entrepreneurial dream includes coming up with exciting new ideas for products and services it will have to wait till another day. There won't be a lot of innovating opportunities for you with most franchises, so forget the idea of selling your homemade cookies along with the nationally-advertised burgers.

The system

With its regulations the franchisor means to protect the brand, making clear how to keep up the company image and style of operating (down to the amount of salt used in each serving of fried potatoes), and exacting fees or other punishment for infractions. The people at franchise headquarters work to make sure no franchisees are likely to do things differently, compromising the familiar aspects of the company's products and services. Such deviation from the expected would put at risk the customer loyalty which a company has nurtured so carefully over the years.

Your operating manual is intended not only for you to know how to preserve the company's good name and reputation but also to provide you with information that will help you run an efficient and profitable operation. Based on the experience of franchisees throughout the system, the rules offer a blueprint for success if you'll just observe them consistently. And if you're stumped by how to carry out some recommended procedure or you're having a problem with one of the employees, you may be able to get a representative from the franchisor to lend a hand either with phone consultation or by getting on an airplane to pay you a visit. Considering their experience of working with other franchisees, these support staff members have seen just about every kind of difficulty you can encounter and will probably offer valuable solutions for your business ills.

But not every franchise is strong in this department. So if you feel you'll want a high level of corporate support from the franchise system you are investigating, talk to some of the franchisees as well as the franchisor representatives. Determine if the company will be committed to your success and find out whether it follows through with its promises.

And keep in mind that you may appreciate a system of rules to follow. If you are someone who finds it reassuring to know that you'll enjoy a high probability of success by carefully adhering to the manual, your best choice may be a franchise with a strong involvement from headquarters.

This idea may not appeal to you, however, if the very reason you decided to go into your own business was to get away from the rules laid down for you by others.

One business buyer listened patiently as a franchise representative talked about the team of experts who swoop down from headquarters in order to aid any franchisee who might need assistance. "You're not alone," the rep explained. "They'll be right there with you, every step of the way. They'll tell you exactly how to reach your goals and how to solve your problems."

But the buyer was unimpressed. "If I felt I wanted someone telling me what to do I'd have kept my corporate job," she explained.

Protected territory

Another double edged sword is the idea that once you've staked your claim with the franchise, your territory will be guarded from incursion by any other franchisee. The area will be yours exclusively. But the flip side is that you can't wander across that boundary into someone else's market. And if your territory is defined in terms of population size there may be no benefit to you if the population continues to grow beyond the numbers guaranteed to you. The franchisor may simply be able to sell another franchise in your territory, arguing that the expanded population warrants a second store. In some parts of California undergoing rapid expansion, this can be a real concern. And if you're worried about it, find out from the franchisor if you will have the right of first refusal for an additional outlet in the area, should the population reach sufficient size.

Even with that permission however, you may feel that your obligation to take on another franchise could cut into your profits. If business is growing quickly for your franchise as you provide Mexican food, photo copy services, muffler replacement or other product or service, you may want to build up the staff so you can continue to meet demand from one location and save overhead. Or you may be willing to open another outlet but not want to buy another "right" from the franchisor.

These are issues to consider as you weigh the benefits and disadvantages in joining a franchise.

And there is the matter of the assessment you'll have to pay in return for your franchise rights.

Franchise fees

The powerful branding, proven operating systems, helpful support staff and protected territories that you enjoy as owner of a franchise come at a price – a percentage of your revenues that go to the franchisor on a regular basis. These costs may well be worth the benefits you enjoy. And as was noted earlier in this section, even the costly advertising budget of a franchisee has its benefits because your message can be conveyed more strongly as part of the collective voice.

As an independent business owner, of course, you would have no such liability. The question is whether as a non-franchise operator you will incur similar costs for marketing, consulting and other business services, and whether you would receive greater value for your dollar as a franchisee or an independent business owner. That's a choice to ponder as you consider the option of joining a franchise.

What Industry is For You?

An important family business conversation held at the kitchen table in the Silicon Valley home of an electronics engineer a few years ago, provides a revealing insight into some of the issues that might be grappled with by someone who wants to buy a business and tries to decide on what industries to explore.

I was privileged to learn about this discussion from Richard who had just been laid off for the third time in four years by a semiconductor manufacturer. The company added employees to design and produce memory and logic circuits when it received new contracts from manufacturers of consumer and business electronics products. Then, once the requests were satisfied, and if there was a slump in new orders – a rather common occurrence in this cyclical industry – the employees would receive two days' notice to clean out their desks and lockers and report to the company's Human Resources Department so they could be terminated.

Richard decided he was no longer willing to stake the financial welfare of his family on the fortunes of the technology business or the whims of the executives in the industry. So his extended family gathered to help him make a decision about what kind of business to buy.

Richard's wife urged him to find a company in the manufacturing sector, preferably in the electronics area, where he could use his education and training. He felt the cost of a company like that would be beyond their budget because so much equipment and materials would be involved.

The plan was to invest $100,000, which would be raised by a home equity loan and a cash infusion from Richard's cousins in Taiwan. They intended to move to California in a year or two and felt that helping to set Richard up in a business, would pay off when they needed his assistance to get established in the U.S.

Richard's uncle recommended the automotive aftermarket industry. He said that it is a growing business in California; everyone has to have a car. And he reminded Richard that he always enjoyed fixing his cars and had a talent for it.

Richard's aunt, who ran a child day care center, felt a service business such as mechanical auto repair or an auto body shop would be a good choice. Her reasoning was that customers have to pay high prices for this work because the business owner has special tools and knowledge. And this results in the owner making a good living.

One of the cousins at the meeting advocated the auto parts business – either importing certain items and selling them to retailers, or purchasing an auto supply retail store that caters to customers fixing their own vehicles. The cousin argued that there always is value in a business which owns a great deal of inventory.

After further discussion and debate, Richard concluded that he wanted to investigate fast food restaurants for sale. This idea didn't sound too promising to Richard's mother. Here's what she said: "You don't know anything about the food business. You can't even toast a slice of bread without almost setting your house on fire."

But Richard's cousin liked his idea. He considered a fast food business to be a retail store selling hamburgers, sodas and fries. And the aunt, who advocated a company in the service sector, argued that fast food is not a product business but a service business. She did agree that it could have a good future as more people were joining the workforce and no one had time to stay home and cook meals.

It took nearly a year of looking at businesses and considering various options (while holding down a couple of part time jobs to feed the family) before Richard finally found a fast food restaurant that met his criteria for price, earnings, location, length of lease and other factors he considered important. The venture proved very successful and within three years he opened two additional locations – one he ran himself, the other was operated by the family members who'd loaned him money to get started.

The business buyer reviewing this story might find some helpful insights in the discussion among Richard and his family members. It shows a typical process of deciding what industry to choose and what kind of business to buy.

Among the options considered were manufacturing, service and wholesale/retail. And the discussion about industries touched on technology, automotive and fast food. It's interesting that Richard's ultimate decision had nothing to do with his background and experience in electronic engineering or with his interests (having to do with cars). Instead he chose a business he knew nothing about – as his mother had reminded him in colorful language – because it seemed to offer a bright, lucrative future.

Someone else, given the same choices, might reach a completely different decision. And how you choose among different types of businesses and industries is entirely up to the priorities you think are most important when you select the areas of businesses to pursue. You may know exactly where you belong without having to review a list of SIC codes and engaging in hours of research as well as self examination. Or perhaps you're completely undecided.

In either event, you will benefit by narrowing your focus – a recommendation offered in the following chapter.

And before you come to that decision, if you haven't yet made up your mind, it might be helpful for you to consider whether you want to be engaged in a familiar industry where your background will come into play. Think also about your interests, then research the kinds of businesses that might match up with things you love to do.

This can be an exciting time for you as it represents an opportunity for major career renewal. The right choice has the potential to give you tremendous rewards, both monetarily and in the satisfaction derived from your work.

Conclusion

Among the choices presented to someone wanting to buy a business is whether that really is a better choice than launching a startup. Assuming the choice is for the purchase of an existing enterprise, you then may select among businesses offering full time participation or part time involvement. You also have a choice as to whether or not to buy a franchise. And then there is the range of issues having to do with the kind of business and industry in which you want to be invested.

KEY POINTS FROM THIS CHAPTER

❖ *If you are interested in purchasing an existing business, you'll learn much about that approach from reading this book.*

❖ *If you're undecided between a business purchase and launching a startup, you'd be well advised, after taking ideas from this book, to get information about starting a new business, available in libraries, chambers of commerce and from a number of business schools. Comparing advice from both sources you then can determine which approach is most appropriate for you.*

❖ *The "absentee business" is probably a misleading concept as all businesses will require some of your time and attention. You may buy a company that requires only part-time involvement, such as a coin operated business, where little or no human contact with customers is needed.*

❖ *If investigating a coin operated or vending business it is important to be extra skeptical about the stated earnings – if anything is stated – because there is little business documentation to support the sales figures.*

❖ *With a few years' of water and utility bills for a laundromat, for example, along with a calculator, you may be able to make a pretty close guess as to actual income. But you should be aware that sellers can still misrepresent the amount of usage by keeping the machines busy, though they are not serving customers.*

❖ *Another important area of choice has to do with the generally lower risk but reduced control a buyer has with a franchised business.*

❖ *It may be safer and easier to follow the operating program provided by the franchisor. But for someone tired of being "told what to do" and someone who wants to maximize profits, the better choice is probably a non-franchise business.*

❖ *Other questions to answer when contemplating a business buying campaign relate to personal choices as to interests, background and perceived future value.*

❖ *Among the industries to consider when determining what kind of company to buy are manufacturing, retail, and service for individuals or businesses.*

❖ *The buyer is advised to begin narrowing the choice so as to be able to focus on the most likely businesses to buy.*

CHAPTER THREE

PREPARATION

"I'm sure there are more difficult things in life than trying to buy a business I just don't know what they might be."

That's the way one buyer explained his year-and-a-half campaign – he called it a "crusade" – to purchase a small California business. The crusade ended successfully when he took over a custom cabinet shop from the founder who was ready to retire after over 40 years in business. And he was right: It wasn't easy.

Still, his assessment may not be accurate – buying a business is not among the most difficult challenges in life. But it is a demanding task filled with frustrations and disappointments, and no guarantee of success. Buyers who've finally discovered a suitable company they were able to purchase have reported conducting their searches for periods ranging from six months to more than two years.

Among the factors making this such a difficult project is the simple reality of demand and supply. More people want to purchase a business with a history of earnings and a positive future than there are available companies fitting that description. Also making this a hard endeavor are the offerings of businesses that seem appealing at first glance but don't maintain that appeal under scrutiny.

And the buyer's search is further complicated by the discovery of unreasonable sellers offering good businesses. Sellers who have an inflated idea about the value of their companies are the other side of the "unrealistic buyers" coin. Some sellers think they'll get more than their business' value from a buyer who has more cash than common sense. The way this plays out is that you'll have your time wasted with business offerings that just don't compute when you examine the numbers. At the right price the math would work out fine; you'd get a reasonable return so you can take a salary and pay off any debt incurred to make the purchase. And sometimes you can wait until a seller comes back "down to Earth." I've seen that strategy employed. But you may not want to have anything to do now, or later, with someone who has insulted you by expecting you to be a sucker.

Buyers who become discouraged after they discover – yet again – that a business which looked so promising is, in fact, a losing proposition, would do well to adjust their disappointment threshold, perhaps become a little more cynical, if they're going to continue the search.

You, the buyer, need to learn – if you haven't already – that the cycle of high hopes followed by sad reality is really just part of the buying process. And you need to continue, undaunted, with your search.

And you should know another major reason your search for the right business is likely to be so difficult – it's because of your unrealistic ideas about what's available.

Realistic Expectations Are Critical

Buyers seem to cherish certain myths about finding the right company and are guided by these falsehoods in the search. One has to do with the perfect business. The danger in setting your sights for the opportunity that will score a 100% match with every single one of your criteria, is that you'll reject businesses that are promising, profitable and priced fairly, while continuing the search for the unrealizable ideal.

I'm not advocating that you settle for a situation that doesn't really work for you. What I am suggesting is that successful buyers are able to replace the wishful thinking with an understanding of the characteristics – good and bad – they're most likely to find in the search for a suitable business to buy.

Another myth that should be dispelled concerns the unsophisticated sellers whom you'll be able to persuade, somehow, to let you have their companies at bargain basement prices. The logic of this reasoning escapes me as I don't understand how an owner with enough business savvy to manage and build a healthy company could be stupid enough to sell it at a discount.

The companion myth is that a buyer who is properly trained can purchase a business with no money down and then use the company's earnings to pay all the debt incurred for the purchase. This concept reminds me of the slight-of-hand demonstrations at which people lose their money by betting on the location of a pea under one of three cups. I suspect the hucksters who conduct – what they call – "seminars" – to teach no-money-down gimmicks are responsible for getting people to believe in this false idea.

A good rule of thumb you can keep in mind concerning any deals offered at a price or terms that seem too good to be true, is that there is some key information on the offering that was left out of the presentation. Keep researching and asking questions and you'll discover the enormous debt that the buyer will be required to assume, or the fact that the operation has been bleeding red ink for years and is actually about to go out of business.

When consulting with a buyer who is looking for a no-money-down deal, or below-market asking price, or some other extraordinary advantage, I usually encourage the client to change his or her approach. If you're looking for a win-lose proposition – that is, you want to gain an unearned benefit in a deal, to the detriment of the other party – my experience tells me you'll be disappointed. The most successful transactions are those in which all participants get what they want, or most of it. And nobody seems to come out ahead if there is an effort, on one or both sides, to take an unfair advantage. That's the lose-lose proposition.

The business buyer most likely to enjoy a successful conclusion for the search campaign is someone focused on finding a healthy business with a good future and a reasonable seller. Your expectations, if they are based on realities of the market and the willingness to pay a fair price and terms, will lead you to a business to buy which meets your criteria – that is if you invest enough time and effort.

If, however, you conceive of your search as a contest to see who's smarter, quicker and more deceptive – you or the seller, you'll be likely to engage in lots of negotiations, tinged with anger and bad feelings, but without a suitable business to show for your efforts.

Can you regard the search as a collaborative effort? You'll be working with your team – lawyer, accountant and broker or agent – and with a seller to reach a mutually desirable goal. With this idea at the foundation of your strategy you'll be most effective.

Communications

Well prepared buyers, in addition to working with realistic expectations, are ready to communicate about what they are looking for – their search criteria – as well as about what they are ready to bring to the right deal. Having been involved in hundreds of transactions – as a buyer, a seller or a broker – I can speak from substantial experience about the frustrations that come up when trying to do business with someone who won't reveal any information about what he or she wants, or has to offer.

As one seller told me: "That guy thinks he's so clever because he's playing his cards close to his chest. He wants me to talk but he's not willing to let me know where he's coming from. I don't know if he's interested or qualified. I don't know if he's even someone I want to do business with."

And he added this point: "There are plenty of good buyers for my business – buyers who are up front about where they stand. I don't have time to play cat-and-mouse games with someone who may not even be serious."

Preparing to be a good communicator also involves setting up the mechanics you'll need to get information and respond quickly. A dedicated phone line – preferably a mobile phone that will reach you anywhere- along with a fax and a dedicated email address are recommended. This way you and your team members are in a position to exchange information quickly and securely. And make sure an answering machine or voice mail is connected to your phone lines so you don't miss any important messages and so that those with whom you are working, know that you're serious about good communications.

Don't be one of those buyers whose 4-year-old answers the phone when a broker is calling to tell you about a situation, new on the market, that might be just what you want. Being prepared so you can exchange information efficiently with team members and with a seller, once you're negotiating, makes it easy for them to conduct business with you. And maintaining good communications increases the chances of your success as a buyer.

Assemble Team

I know of cases where a situation like that described above – a child picks up the phone and sings nursery rhymes to the person calling to tell a buyer about a hot tip on a business – has seriously hampered a buyer's efforts. A similar kind of breakdown occurs when you are one of several prospective buyers for a terrific business, but not in a position to have the financials reviewed or to have a letter of intent drawn up, because you haven't yet established your relationship with the professionals you need to help with the effort.

An important part of your preparation is to interview attorneys – to find one who has experience in business purchases, and to meet with the various accountants you've heard about so you can determine who is best able to quickly examine the books of a small California business and report to you on its condition. You're looking for professionals who are competent at their work, will charge you reasonable rates and – equally important – are people with whom you can work productively. This will, again, require good communication on your end so the working relationship with your advisors gets the desired results with quick turnaround.

Also part of your team should be a few brokers and agents who are in touch with the market of business offerings and can let you know what is available. There's somewhat of an art in dealing with the professionals in business brokerage and we'll get into that subject in more detail in a subsequent chapter. The key point for this discussion is that you want to meet with these people as one of the early steps in your preparation, so they are working on your behalf, trying to find the right business for you to buy. And your good communication with them will enable them to understand what you want and don't want.

Many buyers contact brokers and agents only in response to business-for-sale ads these professionals have listed. If that's your only mode of reaching business sales people, and then you simply ask a few questions and respond to their queries with the predictable comments ("Not interested" or "I'll think about it and let you know if I'm interested)," you're not likely to establish a working rapport with any of those brokers and agents. That means your number will not be entered on their lists of people to contact about interesting new business offerings.

My recommendation is that you interview brokers and agents as you would attorneys and accountants. The difference is that you will work with a single attorney, and one accountant, but may find yourself dealing with a few brokers and agents to help you find a business to buy.

Your Acquisition Resume

And what's one of the first things on the agenda when you meet with a broker or agent? It should be to let them know, with as many specifics as possible, exactly what you are seeking. The best way to do that is with the acquisition resume. It provides a business sales professional with both your criteria and your capabilities in writing, within a single, well organized document.

Does that seem like a lot of trouble? It really is not. You need to collect all your thoughts on this subject anyway. There's probably no better means of communicating what you want and can offer than your acquisition resume.

And I can tell you from the standpoint of the business broker that a document like this will help you immeasurably in gaining the attention and the allegiance of the people with whom you are working. All they have to do is refer to your document to know exactly what will work for you and also to be reminded that you are a favored buyer because you are organized, communicative and clear about objectives.

Similar to the resume used in looking for a job, your acquisition resume will start with the objective, explaining the general type and size of business that you seek. Then it can cover, in more detail, some of the businesses you might like. You can make a list of suitable kinds of companies, and note the industries that will work, as well as your preference for retail, manufacturing, wholesale distribution, or some types of personal or business service firms. How many employees do you want to manage? Are you interested in a business that is open on the weekends? These are topics you should be thinking about and be prepared to note on your document. And be sure to include a list or an explanation of what you don't want. This will make your search criteria even more useful and will help avoid time-wasting introductions to businesses that don't meet your interests or needs.

The next section should let brokers, agents and sellers know about your financial requirements and what size company you are capable of purchasing.

Also in this document you can review your work history and experience, so that anyone reading it would know what you are capable of managing.

The acquisition resume isn't the only part of your campaign that will have similarities to a job search. Many of the things you would do if hunting for a position with a company, governmental agency or other organization, you will do when looking for the right business. It's important, for example, that you make it a habit to network with people who might be able to help, that you pursue all interesting – even just moderately interesting – opportunities, and that you work consistently at your objective until it is realized.

Remember that there are more buyers for good business opportunities than there are good businesses. The market dynamics are similar to that of pursuing a job along with other candidates. As in a job search, the hunt for your business entails a great deal of preparation and forethought.

Financial Preparation

Among the important items on the acquisition resume is the amount of money you are prepared to put into a deal. Let your business sales professionals and any prospective sellers know what you have for a down payment and working capital. And this is the time to decide, and then declare, what personal assets you will use, if any, to secure an obligation incurred as a result of the seller financing part of a deal. If you're adamantly set against anything other than assets of the business being used as collateral for the seller's loan, you should be aware that this will reduce your desirability as a buyer, and limit the number of offerings to which you'll be introduced. You may be thinking that "it depends on the deal." And maybe this indecision helps keep you in your comfort zone. But it doesn't let those with whom you are working know what you are willing to do to get a business. And it makes their job harder.

You don't always have to cover the full amount of the obligation to the seller with collateral. Sometimes he or she will be satisfied with a second trust deed on your home for an amount of say, half the note, with the other half collateralized with assets of the company you are purchasing. Maybe you are willing to do more. Or less. You determine the limits of what you're willing and able to do, and that should be revealed as part of your buyer profile. And regardless of your limits it is important that those invited to do business with you – as your representatives or as the other party in your transaction – are informed of exactly your capabilities and what you are willing to do.

A lender letter is a very useful addition to your acquisition resume. Speak to your business bank to determine how much money it might be willing to lend, based on your assets, credit history and the type of business you are intending to purchase. You're unlikely to get any kind of a solid commitment until the bank execs have a chance to review the financial information – both history and current condition – for the company you're planning to buy. But the bank's interest in working with you can be committed to writing in the form of a preliminary approval, which is the document you would use to demonstrate you're likely to have additional resources to draw on when making the purchase. You'll find more information on financing strategies in a later chapter.

Time is of the Essence

And while a buyer is getting prepared it never hurts to remind himself or herself of the adage that says time is of the essence. Acting quickly and responding decisively can mean the difference between getting the business you want and just missing out on what would have been a great opportunity. So make sure you are prepared to move on any possibility that comes up when you get that phone call in the canned goods aisle of your grocery store, or on the way to your kids' soccer practice or, at the place where you're working until you can find your business and quit the job.

I'm familiar with several situations involving a lost opportunity due to lack of preparation on the part of a buyer – both mental and in terms of the technology needed to communicate promptly and effectively. That's why I advocate the dedicated phone line, the use of message management tools (voice mail or a phone answering system), and even a fax that you can use to send and receive documents in a hurry. Most of the time, a fax machine in your study is simply a dust catching eyesore, incongruent with the rest of the decor in the room. But when you're in the middle of competitive negotiations, the machine's ability to get the seller's information to you and to transmit your letter of intent to her in a few minutes, makes it a most blessed instrument of your victory.

Conclusion

Due to a number of factors: Including the supply and demand imbalance in favor of the seller, the sense of frustration that can set in after a string of disappointments, the number of unsuitable or improperly priced businesses offered, and the unrealistic expectations of many buyers, the discovery and purchase of a desirable small California business is a difficult project to complete successfully. Buyers are advised to be prepared so the quest can be managed effectively. Included in the preparatory steps are assembling a team of support professionals (including attorney, accountant and business sales professionals), putting together an acquisition resume, getting organized with respect to the cash that will be available and might be raised, and being ready and equipped to move quickly if necessary.

KEY POINTS FROM THIS CHAPTER

❖ *The purchase of a profitable small California business with a promising future at a fair price can be a difficult task to complete, due in part to the fact there are more buyers than there are satisfactory businesses on the market.*

❖ *The other side of the "unreasonable buyers" coin are sellers who hope to catch someone willing to meet an excessive asking price. This factor, and the presence of totally unsuitable businesses that should not be offered because they don't make economic sense, can cause a great deal of frustration on the part of buyers who aren't ready for the disappointments that come with this process.*

❖ *For a buyer to be successful at finding a suitable business it is critical that he or she is realistic about what is available and at what price. Buyers "holding out" for the perfect opportunity risk missing out on perfectly good deals, while waiting for the "ideal" business.*

❖ *Another error buyers make is to assume that they can purchase a business at a below-market rate or with unrealistic terms, such as no money down. By approaching the market with these ideas, buyers are more likely to waste time and burn their bridges with brokers, agents and sellers, than they are to buy a suitable business.*

❖ *Buyers who wish to be successful at finding and purchasing a suitable business are urged to communicate effectively with advisors, business sales professionals and sellers. Those who don't explain precisely what they want and what they can do will be unable to build the alliances and trust needed to reach their objective.*

❖ *Part of communicating well is having the mechanics in place, including a mobile phone, a way to receive and to access phone messages, and a fax machine readily available.*

❖ *The time to build your team of professionals – attorney, accountant and business sales professionals – is at the beginning of your search. That way you won't be caught un-prepared if you need to move quickly on an interesting deal.*

❖ *The acquisition resume, which details a buyer's search criteria as well as his or her capabilities – financial and otherwise – is a very effective way to communicate with brokers, agents and sellers. It should include what the buyer is not interested in so as to be as explicit as possible.*

❖ *Buyers are well advised to provide some detail of their financial strength, including how much cash is available for down payment and working capital, how much in the way of assets will be used as collateral for seller financing (assuming the buyer is willing to pledge, for example, some real estate equity), and how much might be obtained from the buyer's bank if the deal is acceptable to the lender.*

❖ *The search for a good business to buy can be compared to a job search. There are more good candidates to buy a business than there are suitable businesses, just as there may be several applicants for a position with a company, government agency or other organization.*

❖ *Time is of the essence in many cases when buyers are competing for a desirable business. That's why a buyer is smart to be prepared to move quickly and decisively on an opportunity, if the occasion warrants. And a well prepared buyer is in a position to use all of the modern communications technology at his or her disposal to facilitate rapid and effective communication.*

HOW TO LOCATE AVAILABLE BUSINESSES

Despite what you may have heard there is no secret to finding a small California business for sale that will meet your needs.

Well, there is, if you consider the idea of "working hard to achieve your objective" a secret.

Like the comparison with a job search that was applied to preparation in the previous chapter, the process of locating a business you want to buy is quite similar to what you'd do when hunting for satisfactory employment. There are traditional sources to explore in electronic and print classified ads, advisors to work with, and the more resourceful techniques, such as cold calling on targets of interest.

And, just as with a job search, there is no "best" way to find a suitable business. You are advised to do a little of everything – formal and informal procedures. Be prepared for your business search to take anywhere from six months to two years – longer than most job hunts.

On-Line Listings

The chief source of listings and information about small California businesses for sale – and thus the most popular traditional strategy – is the Internet, where data banks list everything from the simplest, low-investment opportunities (how about a nice shoe shine stand?) to offerings with several employees and prices that reach the maximum value for a small California business – about $5 million.

One useful resource for finding opportunities is the bizben.com site because of the speed and easy access to so many businesses being offered – hundreds of new listings are added each week, and because of the wealth of information, ideas and other resources that also reside on the site. It is reached at *www.bizben.com*

The site allows buyers to organize their search for available businesses according to type of business, geographic area, or by using the advanced search mode to hunt for offerings using key words. You'll also see photos accompanying featured businesses on the site.

This is, perhaps, the leading resource for small businesses being sold in California, as it is responsible for connecting dozens of buyers and sellers throughout the state every week. Incidentally, the site produces a companion print newsletter which includes listings and other editorial material of use to business buyers. It can be ordered from the bizben.com website.

Classified Ads in Print

Until a few years ago when the Internet took over as the prime repository of classified listings – serving scores of industries and all kinds of consumer and business interests – the chief resource for buyers was the classified ad pages of their local newspapers. All of the metropolitan dailies in California provide listings of businesses for sale.

While most offerings of small California businesses are posted online, you'll find some opportunities advertised only in print. And the newspapers still serve buyers who don't have easy and anytime access to the Internet. I've noticed that most of the newspaper advertising of business opportunities appears in the Sunday editions. So that's the day to check the classifieds for businesses for sale – or listed as business opportunities – in most papers covering large California cities.

The other way to find classified ads for companies being offered is by searching in the trade magazines covering those industries which most interest you. This takes a bit more time and effort than going on-line or opening your newspaper. Still, it's a good strategy if you want to focus on a specific business that might not get promoted in other media.

A few years ago a plumber in Los Angeles suffered a back injury and was unable to continue in the trade. He received disability insurance payments but needed more income. He had the idea to find out if there were any plumbing supply businesses for sale in his area. There were no listings on line or in the L.A. papers for such a business, but he did find one advertised for sale in a trade periodical to which he subscribed.

The best way to pursue this strategy may be to identify a few businesses in which you have a particular interest. Then obtain the industry-specific publications that are read by those in the targeted businesses. Your public library has a directory of these periodicals you can use to find the appropriate publications.

Another place to find these publications as well as possible "for sale" notices is at the offices of the associations that represent the businesses which you'd like to target in your search efforts. There's a wealth of information to be obtained from this source. A check of the yellow pages in your telephone book under "associations," "business and trade organizations," "chambers of commerce", "women's organizations" and "labor organizations" will give you the information you need to contact dozens of these offices. And they may have their own publications, bulletin boards or even a knowledgeable person you can talk with to get information about who, in their business, wants to retire, and how to learn more about the person's company.

Residents of heavily populated areas in California will find enough of these organizations to stay busy for months. The pickings will be slimmer for residents of the state's rural sections, but you still can call or email these resources at their metropolitan locations to start a dialog and receive their newsletters and other information that can lead you to businesses being offered.

Business Brokers and Agents

If you don't find a business you like using the more traditional sources, you undoubtedly will notice some advertising from business sales professionals – brokers or agents. They not only offer an abundance of information about what's available, they can help direct you to the opportunities that make the most sense based on your interests and abilities. At least the good brokers and agents can do that. Your research among the brokers offering business for sale will likely take several unexpected turns, as the people you talk to may want to switch you to something other than what you contacted them about. That's all right if your broker contact understands your wants, needs and abilities, and doesn't try to persuade you to buy something that *he* or *she* thinks is the best deal.

With helpful representatives, you will have quick access to information about businesses that may be just right for you. If you draw the short straw, however, by connecting with someone – for example, as a result of your phone call in response to an ad – who is neither knowledgeable nor dedicated to client service, you may have your time wasted. We'll go into some detail, in the following chapter, about how you can find, evaluate and select the business sales professionals who can aid you the most.

Advertising for Businesses

If you happen to have, among your personality traits, the first characteristic mentioned in the description of a successful business owner, back in Chapter One, then you won't be content to wait for the right business to appear in the classified ads. And you won't just sit at home, hoping that you'll get a call from a member of your team of business brokers and agents to alert you about a promising opportunity.

Among the proactive steps you can take is to write ads for yourself, letting prospective sellers know about your capabilities and your interest in talking to them if they're ready to sell. These ads can be placed in the same locations where you find businesses being offered, including Internet and printed classifieds. And if you would like to be notified when a specific kind of business becomes available in your area, you might be able to pay to post a notice in the office of the association that represents the target industry. Or advertise in the industry association's newsletter.

Some of the main points listed in your acquisition resume belong in your ad. And it can be worded like one of the following:

Example 1

Wanted to buy: Manufacturing business with annual sales in the range of $1 million to $10 million. Have $250,000 cash for down payment, $200,000 real estate equity, and access to additional funds for working capital. Substantial business management experience. Contact (name and contact information).

Example 2

Cash buyer has $100,000 down payment for distribution or retail business with history of steady earnings and seller willing to train. Have business experience and bank line of credit. Contact (name and contact information).

Example 3

Attention business owners ready to retire: Serious buyer for your company with as much as $125,000 in cash and bank credit. Will respect your confidentiality. Please, no franchises. Contact (name and contact information).

Example 4

Ready to buy your restaurant. Have cash and food service experience. Will consider unprofitable businesses if fairly priced with good lease. Contact (name and contact information).

Include Advisors and Vendors

And don't stop with your ad campaign. You can extend your search to the inner sanctum where the decision to sell is formulated. By contacting attorneys and account-ants, you are going right to the source – the people who would be first to know about any retirement planning by business owners among their clientele. Having done this – attempting to get in with some business attorneys and CPAs – I discovered that while many of them are reluctant to take the time to sit down with someone who isn't a source of immediate business, they are willing to set up a file for your letter and contact information. And some took my calls when I phoned to remind them to tell their clients about my interests.

It took a while before I got a response using this technique, and I was disappointed about the quality of businesses offered. But the exercise demonstrated that this could be a good source of leads if a buyer continues to work with it.

And while you're at it, contact some of the vendors in your targeted businesses. They frequently learn when an owner is ready to sell. In fact, there are times when a supplier is aware that one of his or her customers needs to sell before the customer does.

An example of this was demonstrated when Sam, a recent immigrant living in Central California, made the rounds of the wholesale food distributors in his area to let them know he and his family wanted to own a grocery store. He provided each with a copy of his acquisition resume stating how much money he had and detailing his experience in the business.

This clever tactic was almost immediately successful. The manager for one of the packaged foods warehouses introduced Sam to an elderly man, who because of an illness was unable to keep his convenience store open during the long hours needed to accommodate customers. The deal that resulted was a win-win-win as it allowed the seller to retire, provided the new owner with a business to work in and build up with his family, and allowed the warehouse manager to replace a poor customer with a new one who did more business and made larger purchases.

A strategy like this can apply to most any industry. The wholesale suppliers, equipment providers and business-to-business services that work with companies in your area of interest are familiar with everyone in their territory. These vendors know who is successful, who is preparing to retire, and who is doing an inadequate job of managing a business and should turn it over to more competent ownership.

Every route driver and sales person can be a potential scout for you, as each of them knows anyone in the territory who might be a suitable seller. There is no reason you can't pay a finder's fee for someone who puts you on to the right lead.

I like this approach because it makes the buyer an "insider." Have you ever learned about a good business that you might have bought, had you known it was for sale, but it went to someone "on the inside" before the seller even had a chance to offer the company to the market? The insider can be you, if you get yourself known as a serious buyer in the industry and you can show how there will be a benefit for anyone able to introduce you to the right opportunity.

A Guerrilla Campaign at the Source

Any reason you can't do what business brokers and agents do when they go on cold calling safaris? If you think you'd like to own the business where you bring your dry cleaning, pick up imported cheeses, or browse for books and magazines, and the proprietor looks like he needs a vacation, just ask if there might be an interest in selling to you. Have a copy of your acquisition resume to hand over so the business owner can give the idea some thought and contact you if interested.

Keep in mind, if you're doing this, that most business owners are fearful about their employees learning that they want to sell. That's because once the word gets out, employees may move on, and some customers may feel less loyal and start frequenting the competitor's business. So find a way to take up the subject discretely with the seller when you approach him about this idea.

The plan can apply to professional practices also. So if you're a dentist, an architect or a CPA, you can contact people in the industry to learn if any have an interest in retiring.

Some buyers I've worked with used sophisticated marketing methods such as mail campaigns targeted at companies they thought might be interesting. You can start implementing this strategy by conducting a little research at your local public library. Get a directory of local businesses and you'll be able to get some valuable data, including the description of the business, address and phone number information, number of employees and owner's name. Some of these resources even list annual sales and the company's credit rating.

The information is not all accurate, so don't rely on the circumstances of the target company being exactly what is reported in the directory. This means if you're putting together a target list of companies with five to ten employees, you might include those listed with 15 or 20 employees. An interesting company listed with sales of $2 million a year in sales should probably be contacted, even if you don't think you're interested in any business that doesn't reach at least $5 million in annual revenue.

What I have seen work successfully is the use of a simple postcard for the mailing, which invites the recipient to call you if interested in talking about the sale to you of his or her business. Give your contact information. You might want to add some statements that will make your "pitch" more persuasive. Point out that you will respect the business owner's request for confidentiality, that you are not a broker soliciting for listings, and that you are willing to pay a fair price for a good business.

You can follow up with a bunch of phone calls to the more interesting of the prospects on your list. Speak directly to the owner and let him or her know that you understand this might not be a good time for them to speak. Ask when you can call back or if they would prefer to call you. If they are not interested, perhaps they know someone – a colleague or neighbor – in a similar business who is ready to retire. Tell the person about your finder's fee program and ask if you should send your acquisition resume.

And you can go door-to-door in industrial parks, where you'll find service as well as distribution and manufacturing businesses. I know the idea of cold calling like that makes some people feel squeamish. You can take heart in the knowledge that since you aren't calling on the business owner to sell something – in fact you want to be the customer – you might get a pleasant reception. Provide your acquisition resume and ask for referrals to other possible acquisition candidates if the person you're speaking with isn't interested.

Remember the importance of discretion. One of the business brokers who practices cold calling in search of listings knows that business owners don't want to be seen, by employees, talking to a business broker. So this broker is very careful in the way she approaches this project. She learns the names of owners from one of the business directories mentioned above, then asks for the person by name when she enters the place of business. She never reveals her business affiliation when she is greeted by the receptionist or customer service person. She explains that her visit with the owner will take only a moment and that it is a personal matter. And she says "I'm not here to sell anything."

Then if she can meet with the owner briefly, she explains who she is and how she may be able to assist. Then she tells the owner: "I realize this is not the time or place to discuss this. When would be convenient for us to meet off premises or speak privately on the phone about how I can help you sell?"

And if she is unable to get a quick, private chat with the owner – either the person is not there or refuses to give her the time – she follows with a phone call or a letter with its envelope addressed by hand and marked "confidential." She usually explains the reason for her contact in these private communications, but never leaves a message in the general voice mailbox when she phones.

The broker is quite successful at obtaining listings with this technique. Her strategy is to try a few times to contact the owner – using an unannounced visit, phone call or personal letter – at least enough so the seller knows she wants to speak with him or her and why.

"If I can't make contact with them," she says, "I take that to mean they aren't interested. But if I do hear back, they usually appreciate the professional way that I conduct myself."

A buyer interested in contacting prospective sellers of small businesses would do well to incorporate her approach.

Conclusion

Finding a small California business to buy can be a challenge, not unlike finding the right job, although locating a suitable business might require more time than it takes to land a good job.

There are various strategies that can be employed to uncover a willing seller of a suitable company, and the prospective buyer is advised to consider all of them, and use as many as possible so as to have several things working at once. These strategies include the simplest, which is accessing business-for-sale want ads on-line and in print, to the most guerrilla-like methods of cold calling and advertising for businesses to buy.

Business brokers and agents can be an excellent resource and the following chapter covers some details about working with them.

One suggestion is to cold call on businesses and speak to the owners. This can be productive, but is a strategy that must be handled carefully, so that employees and customers don't catch on to what you're doing. A few tips offered by someone successful at this technique are included to help you use this approach successfully.

KEY POINTS FROM THIS CHAPTER

❖ *Finding a business can be compared to the hunt for a job in terms of the fact that there are several ways to go about it, and the best strategy is to employ as many means as possible.*

❖ *The most common method of locating businesses for sale is the researching of on-line listings. Among the most widely used Internet resource for small businesses in California is www.bizben.com, which is responsible for matching dozens of buyers and sellers in the state every month.*

❖ *Before on-line sources were available, the number one destination for people investigating businesses for sale was the listings that appeared in newspaper classified advertising sections. These still can help you uncover some offerings which may not be posted on line. And printed classifieds provide a resource for those who don't have ready access to the Internet.*

❖ *The Sunday editions of the metropolitan newspapers in California include, in their classified sections, the ads for local businesses for sale. You'll find these sections in editions published during the week, but they don't have nearly as many listings as those that come out every Sunday.*

❖ *Printed classifieds also can be found in trade periodicals and are recommended for those who want to research available businesses in targeted industries. Your public library has directories in which you can find industry-specific publications for this purpose.*

❖ *Business brokers and agents – if you work with ones who are competent – are a very good source of information about businesses for sale, and can help you to negotiate for, and to purchase a company that you want to own.*

❖ *Among the more pro-active techniques is to run your own "business wanted" ads in an on-line service or in a trade periodical that focuses on an industry which you want to target.*

❖ *Business advisors and vendors are an excellent source of information regarding whom, among their clients, may want to sell. Someone providing goods or services to other businesses usually knows a great deal about those enterprises, how successful they are, and whether the current owner would benefit by selling out.*

❖ *Business advisors, such as attorneys and accountants, are the first people to know when the business owners among their clients want to retire or sell for other reasons. Providing your acquisition resume to these professionals is another possible way to uncover a good business for sale.*

❖ *Consider offering a finder's fee to someone who can direct you to a seller whose business you purchase.*

❖ *Also recommended as a pro-active method is launching a mail campaign to business owners, explaining your interest in learning if they want to sell.*

❖ *This same approach, but conducted in person, can be effective if handled in such a way as to respect a seller's concern for confidentiality. Don't tell the receptionist who greets you that you want to buy the business, only that you have a "brief and personal" matter to discuss with the owner.*

CHAPTER FIVE

HOW TO CHOOSE A BUSINESS BROKER OR AGENT TO HELP YOU BUY A BUSINESS

One of my favorite business broker stories concerns an engineer in Southern California who was looking at businesses to buy, because he'd been laid off, and happened to tell a broker he'd always wanted to own a hardware store just like the one in the town where he lived.

"I've been bugging the owner to sell to me," the engineer said to the broker. "I've gone in there several times – both as a customer and to find out if he's ready to sell. He always tells me to come back in a few weeks. But every time I follow up with him he says he's not ready yet."

"He probably doesn't want to sell," the broker suggested, "but if you're a customer, he's reluctant to come out and say 'no' to you."

"He's up there in age. I think he should sell," the engineer noted.

"Well I'll be glad to talk to him," the broker suggested.

"You can try," the engineer said. "But I doubt you'll get anywhere."

A week later the broker called his client to report he had a listing on the store, and after some negotiations between the buyer and seller for the next few days, a buy/sell agreement was finalized.

While chatting with the retiring hardware store owner a few days before close of escrow, the engineer asked him: "Why didn't you want to sell to me when I asked you. Now, with the broker involved, you have to pay a commission."

"I guess you're right," the older man said. "The thing is, I just didn't know how to answer you. I wanted to tell you I was ready to sell, but I didn't know how to go about it – the ins and outs of selling. Then I talked to the broker, he said he could handle everything – that I didn't have to worry about how to sell to you."

"But, we could have had a contract written up by someone else, maybe your attorney or mine," the engineer observed.

"I hate dealing with attorneys if you don't have to" the hardware store owner said. "Usually it costs a lot of money – about $100 for every 'wherefore' and 'therefore' – and then you've got to sign on the dotted line without really knowing what you're getting yourself into.

"No," the seller concluded. "It's better this way."

What this points out, I think, is that there is a legitimate and a vital role that business brokers can play in bringing about a deal.

Brokers, Agents, Brokerages

Before discussing that role, a quick review is in order to help those readers, unfamiliar with California brokerage law, to understand the basic distinctions in discussing buyers' representatives.

Licensed by the State of California under real estate law, business *brokers* and *agents* are required to know about the basics of contracts, negotiations, escrow, financing and related matters. And to be successful in this specialty, they should have a firm grounding in the disciplines of business accounting and of marketing.

The total of the two categories of licensees – brokers and agents – is about 900 people throughout the state. Most of them formally represent sellers, with a listing agreements serving as their agency contract. Most also work with buyers as a function of their responsibilities to selling clients. Some represent buyers only for a fee.

A broker licensed by the state of California can conduct real estate, business opportunities transactions and related activities and supervise other licensees who do the same under the broker's license. Those supervised are usually agents who also are licensed, but under less stringent requirements compared to brokers. The broker is required to approve all agreements such as listings and sales contracts, in which he or she is involved, either as active participant or as supervisor, and has responsibilities for the legality and proper execution of these agreements. Brokers can be liable for illegal, improper or unethical practices. Agents also can be liable if their practices violate California law or code of ethics.

Brokerage is a company established to provide services in the real estate, business opportunities and related markets. Every brokerage is required to have a licensed broker as an employee, owner or officer.

It might also be noted that a licensed California attorney is authorized to perform many of the duties of a broker.

The term broker in this discussion means the legal representative of the seller – either a broker or an agent working under the supervision of a broker, with whom the buyer has most contact.

How Business Brokers and Agents Can Help You

A lot of buyers think it's a "no-brainer" to find a good business and then complete a purchase. I've had people tell me that all you need is a bit of common sense and to be willing to work at it a little. And then the rest is easy.

But I think it's important to remember that a competent and experienced broker has a great deal of knowledge about procedure and law that almost no lay person could have. Most buyers don't have a clue about everything they need to do, and need to understand, when they're trying to buy – even a simple, low cost enterprise.

And then what about the expertise that business brokers and agents develop over their months – and years – of working with buyers and sellers, landlords, lenders, franchisors and governmental agencies? That's important know-how that you aren't likely to just figure out or pick up by talking to someone who's bought a business.

Most important are the resources business brokers and agents have at their disposal for use in helping buyers. Business sales professionals have immediate access to listings of businesses for sale, and the information about them, through their brokerages. Their other valuable resources can include lenders (if extra cash is needed to close escrow), inventory services that are quick and reasonable in their rates, business valuation professionals who know the market and understand how it influences value, equipment appraisers, and escrow holders who have special expertise with particular kinds of transactions.

Knowledgeable business sales professionals have all this and more in their phone directories. And I know of instances when a call to the right one of these resources has helped to save a deal that was at risk of going "belly up."

Most buyers are well served by competent representation from the brokerage community. This support can start when someone is first contemplating the idea of buying a company, and needs a way to understand and to work with the market. Then it can extend all the way through the close of escrow, and beyond.

Despite these reasons, there are some of you in the community of buyers for small California businesses who insist you'd rather do it yourself. Perhaps you're imbued with the spirit that fills many entrepreneurs, and results in the habit of independent thinking and extreme self sufficiency. If this is you, my question is: Why not do both?

Go ahead and continue looking for just what you want, talking to owners and sellers, and evaluating the available offerings, while relying on only your own resources and business experience to back you up. But while doing that, interview some brokers and get an idea if there is anyone in the field who can be of assistance.

In fact, you might want to be aware of some of the little-known ways that you can benefit from a good relationship with a business broker or agent. One way is to have access to offerings that aren't generally known about in the marketplace.

Pocket listing or "fill an order"

The "pocket listing," for example, is the authority a business sales professional has obtained to offer a business for sale, but is not actively promoting. The seller's intense concerns for confidentiality may be the reason that it isn't advertised or made available to other brokers. Perhaps that business is exactly what you've been looking for.

And if the broker with whom you're working can't offer an interesting business proposition to consider, you might want to give him or her an order to fill. Just describe your ideal business in as much detail as possible and the broker can try and match that request by conducting research in the business directories covering your target area.

The broker's strategy is to approach owners of the companies that might meet your criteria, with an explanation that is expressed something like this: "I have a client (that's you) who would be interested in purchasing your business." As you might guess, the brokers are rebuffed in most cases. And in some situations they can't even get access to the owner to have that conversation. Indeed, this soliciting activity can entail a lot of work.

But many brokers are skilled at this procedure, with various strategies for getting the owner's attention and – once that attention is obtained – for getting the person to talk with some candor.

And the brokers know their statistics. Small California businesses change hands, on average, every five years. That means that each approach to an owner has one chance in five of turning up a positive. Or, put another way, if a broker can approach 20 owners about the idea of selling, the odds dictate that four of them either have their business on the market or are planning to do so.

This campaign, presumably on your behalf, is an effective way for a broker to obtain a listing – the written authorization from a business owner to offer the business for sale at specified price and terms, with the understanding that the owner will pay a commission (the amount or percentage is specified) to the broker upon a successful sale.

One-party listing

In many cases, the owner's response is articulated in the following way: "I'm not ready to list with you, but if you tell this buyer about my business, and if the buyer is willing to buy it according to my price and terms, then I will sell it to the person and pay your commission." What follows is an agreement called the "One-party listing." This is an authorization to sell, but only to the one person named in the listing.

This type of listing gives the owner the feeling of maintaining control over the marketing of the business, gives the broker an opportunity to put a deal together, and gives you – if you are the person named in the one-party listing – an opportunity to buy a company that might meet your needs.

What's particularly good for you is that this benefit – an interesting business offering for you to consider – comes without any effort on your part. It was the broker who had to do the considerable amount of work to get that one-party listing.

And if these procedures seem too imprecise for your taste, you can hire a broker to approach the owner of a specific business you have in mind, after promising the broker that you'll pay a commission – in this case a finder's fee – in the event you are successful in purchasing the company.

Broker to pre-screen offerings

Another way to use your broker is to get him or her to help with the analysis of businesses that have been brought to you for consideration. One complaint about some brokers and agents is that they present companies for sale that have serious defects – such as short-term lease, priced too high, unattractive sales terms, declining industry – without apology or explanation. A serious buyer, after being invited to look at some of these as possible acquisitions, might conclude: "If that's the best this so-called professional can offer, I'm better off without a broker; certainly without this one."

The solution, of course, is to tell the broker to do some preparatory analysis of any business before it's brought to you. If he or she knows you become impatient with offerings that don't make sense, you'll be presented with fewer listings to consider, with less of your time wasted. And when you are introduced to a business offering, it will have passed at least initial scrutiny.

I know buyers who expect their brokers to run an ROI (return on investment) analysis, cash flow projection, market survey and risk assessment on any business possibility brought to them for consideration. This not only reduces the volume of time-wasting offerings for a buyer to see, it also saves the time and trouble of conducting preliminary research on even the good offerings.

Beware, however, of the danger that a really good business for sale may get connected with another buyer before your broker has had a chance to do the work needed to bring it to you. You may lose a suitable acquisition candidate this way. And you'd better check the broker's work from time to time, to make sure the material you are presented is accurate and complete.

The smart business buyer, then, usually sees advantages in letting business brokers and agents do one of the things they do best – find and present business opportunities for sale – for the benefit of their clients.

You'll do well, in fact, to work with a few brokers – perhaps three or four – so that you'll gain exposure to more listings. Unlike the housing market where every listing is typically available for anyone in the system to sell, the business brokerage field is quite fragmented. Professionals within one brokerage sell only their company's listings and decline to share the listings with other brokerages. This is not a universally popular way of doing things, and you may wonder if a brokerage really represents the best interests of its seller clients when it declines to share its listings with other firms.

Whether this practice is right or wrong, it remains a fact of life in the business. And for a buyer it means your best strategy is to work with more than one brokerage, so as to be exposed to more listings. There may be more time spent initially while you interview, qualify and then select your representatives. But this investment will likely pay off as you'll then have the brokers notifying you of any opportunities they know about which might meet your requirements. Your time can be spent in your own research. This is an efficient way to work, provided you have selected capable brokers and/or agents.

Pay to complete

Some buyers believe in using a third party to help with negotiations. If you've found a business worth buying, and it was through your own efforts, you and the seller can look forward to closing your deal without having a portion of the sales price going to a broker for creating the match-up (of you and the seller). But that assumes you'll be able to make a deal and work out all the details so you can take over the company. What if you can't? It's that worry which motivates some buyers to hire a broker who'll be responsible to handle negotiations and follow up an accepted offer with all the tasks necessary to get the agreement through a completed escrow.

Attorneys also offer this service, but may not have the skills at the ready as would a broker who's accustomed to negotiating the sale of small California businesses with regularity. The deal to strike is that the broker only gets paid – and usually it would be a flat fee – if he or she is successful in getting you and the seller to agree on terms of a purchase, and then is able to manage the transaction until it closes.

Characteristics to Look for In a Broker or Agent

How does one select correctly? There are a number of professionals in the business who are committed to a high level of customer service and honest dealing. But the business also attracts individuals who are drawn to the action – the wheeling and dealing aspect of the business – and who see inexperienced buyers and sellers as potential targets of their little schemes.

Interested in helping you achieve your objectives

In most cases a broker or agent earns a commission by selling a business – the money coming from the seller's proceeds. And California law states that the business sales professional is an agent of the seller. What these facts suggest is that any work a broker or agent does for you, the buyer, is performed only in the hopes of selling you a business and collecting a commission from the business' seller.

Is this why some buyers have a hard time trusting business brokers?

And yet as a practical matter, the brokers and agents who are effective working with buyers are able to focus on the needs of those "clients," earning their trust, arguing on their behalf during negotiations, and making sure the buyer is protected all the way through the close of an escrow.

That's the kind of broker you want. So it's important that anyone wishing to sell a business to you begins this process by asking what you want, and then listening to the answer.

You should be able to discern rather quickly whether the broker you are interviewing is paying attention to your explanation of what you want, or is simply nodding the head and waiting for you to finish talking so you can listen to what he or she wants to tell you about the brokerage's latest listings.

Do the offerings presented to you reflect the criteria you've outlined or is the broker just offering you whatever they're trying to sell? Do you have to point out the deficiencies in proposed businesses or does the broker say something akin to: "I'm not going to tell you about the distribution company because the asking price is much too high?" Does the broker ask more questions about your interests to clearly understand, in detail, your criteria?

Notice how much interest the broker has in your requirements and how much attention is paid to your questions and comments. It's an important clue as to whether the broker or agent is interested in really representing you.

If you're not convinced the person's foremost objective is to determine exactly what you want and then try and get if for you, it's best to strike him or her from your list and work with somebody else.

Has expertise in the field

It should be noted however, that a buyer is not well served by a representative who merely carries out instructions, no matter how well. While understanding what you want and trying to satisfy that, your broker should talk things over with you, telling you if he or she thinks you are unrealistic about your expectations and letting you in on facts or information you may not have.

Whenever you make an offer to purchase a business, you'll want the broker to have some skill at presenting your position forcefully, and the ability to press for the things that are important to you. You won't be present during all the negotiations taking place between the seller and the brokers involved, so don't you want to be confident that the person representing you is arguing persuasively on your behalf? And if your representative has some experience, he or she will be able to cite the facts to prove that you are a strong buyer and that your offer might represent the seller's best deal.

Such positions sometimes draw an argument from the seller's representative who wants to posture for a higher price and better terms. And you'll be at a disadvantage when the brokers are attempting to hammer out a deal if your representative can be "outgunned" due to a lack of experience in this area.

You also want your broker to have some skills at business analysis. Even though I know a great deal about analyzing a set of business records, and about evaluating how a company will perform in the future – based on its infrastructure and the marketplace in which it functions – I still find it valuable to get the feedback from other brokers, to learn if they have a different way of evaluating the business offering under scrutiny. There always is something to learn, and the benefit of having a savvy broker is that you have someone with whom to discuss your ideas, to provide you market intelligence and to offer additional information.

Someone you can trust

It hardly seems worth mentioning that it's critical your broker be someone who is honest and ethical. That should be obvious. And yet I've noticed that people sometimes overlook the tendency on the part of their representative to exaggerate or to tell people "what they want to hear." There's a certain amount of this behavior going on throughout the business world – in most industries – and perhaps we just take it for granted.

But it is wrong. A buyer who wants to be properly represented, should take care not to get involved with a representative who isn't 100% above-board.

I was reminded about this concern recently in talking to a broker who described an agent in his company – an energetic person with a persuasive way of presenting an idea – as "the kind of guy you have to keep on a short leash." That means to me that the person cannot be relied on to give complete, honest and accurate information.

Apparently, this broker is willing to tolerate an employee who has selling skill but comes up short in the ethics department. The person wouldn't work for me as long as a single minute past the time I learned he couldn't be trusted.

And I think that having a completely honest representative should be a concern to you, not only because the information you receive should be factual and unembellished, but also because you could be penalized if your representative makes inaccurate statements about you, or what you want, to a seller. You might call it "stretching the truth" or "putting a spin" on the facts, but the word for it in the California Commercial Code is "misrepresentation." The law says that if a seller suffers damages because he or she relied on statements made by your representative, and those statements were misrepresentations of the facts, you could share liability for the dishonesty of the broker or agent.

Conclusion

Whether or not a buyer is knowledgeable about the process of finding and acquiring a small California business, it's useful to have one or more brokers or agents working on your behalf. Although they are paid out of the seller's funds at close of escrow, many know how to give their true allegiance to a buyer they are representing on a particular offering.

If you are introduced to a specific company by a business sales professional, it will be in that person's interest to make sure you get your questions answered and that you have his or her complete support and assistance if you decide to make an offer to buy it. Some independent-minded buyers prefer to look for business opportunities without benefit of a representative helping out. Others have built up a little team of representatives, one from each of different brokerages, so the buyer has access to the listings of several companies.

In evaluating broker candidates, make sure they have your interests foremost on their agenda – not just an interest in having you agree to buy the latest "hot deal" that has been listed by their brokerage. Other qualities to look for are experience, knowledge and honesty.

KEY POINTS FROM THIS CHAPTER

❖ *The story about a business broker able to get an Exclusive Right to Sell listing from a hardware store owner, even though a customer couldn't get the owner interested in selling, helps to point out that business brokers and agents fill a special and valued role.*

❖ *All business brokers and agents are licensed by the California Department of Real Estate, and must comply with various regulations, including passing tests given by the department. The requirements are more stringent for brokers than for agents. Brokers are responsible for their own actions, of course, and for the actions of the agents under their supervision.*

❖ *A broker or agent can help a buyer with the challenging tasks of finding and negotiating to purchase a business. And while some buyers prefer to work without brokers, feeling that a representative's true allegiance is always to the seller, most brokers are able to work in the interests of a buyer who is their client.*

❖ *One good reason to work with a business sales professional is to benefit from the skill, knowledge and experience acquired by the person. Another is to gain access to the broker's resources such as the listings of businesses for sale, and the referrals to lenders, escrow holders, and other specialists whose expertise is useful for a buyer.*

❖ *Buyers who feel they prefer working on their own, without benefit of assistance from a broker, are advised that they can continue to conduct their individual search, and also get in touch with a few brokers to see what they can offer.*

❖ *If you insist that brokers not waste your time with listings which have serious deficiencies, it will encourage agents and brokers who want to work with you to show you only good opportunities, and to do much of the research and analysis on each offering you see.*

❖ *A little-known benefit to a buyer of having a good relationship with a business broker or agent is the opportunity to learn of a "pocket listing." This is a business which the broker has authority to sell, but is not promoting aggressively. If it is an offering with a great deal of merit, the buyer –being one of the few people who knows about it – would face little competition in his or her bid to purchase the company.*

❖ *The One-party listing is an authorization to sell a business, obtained by a broker, but only to a single individual who is named in the listing. A buyer can ask a broker to try and get such an agreement from the owner of a business the buyer might like to acquire.*

❖ *An important quality of a business broker with whom a buyer wants to work, is attentiveness to the buyer's needs and interests. Some brokers do this well, others pretend to be interested but want only to have the buyer purchase one of the listings currently available from the broker's company.*

❖ *Among the characteristics a buyer should look for in a broker are the experience obtained and the skill developed after working in the business for at least a few years.*

❖ *Buyers should avoid brokers – no matter how clever and charming – who seem to embellish the truth and spin the facts. This person is likely to get the buyer in trouble, in addition to failing to provide him or her with useful service.*

CHAPTER SIX

HOW TO WORK WITH YOUR BROKER OR AGENT

The danger in applying some of the ideas reviewed in the last chapter is that the reader might want to stop there, thinking that's all you have to do – select a few outstanding brokers or agents to hunt for good acquisition candidates for you. Then, you just wait to see what they've discovered for you to review.

As was pointed out, putting business sales professionals to work for you, in your hunt for a company to buy, is an excellent strategy. And selecting the individuals with integrity and with the experience and the resources to do a good job is part of that strategy. But only part.

For them to be effective in searching out opportunities, perhaps following leads you supply, and presenting you with quality offerings worth investigating, brokers and agents need to be provided with plenty of information about what you want, and what you can do. And they need heavy doses of honest communication and a cooperative attitude so they're encouraged to persist on your behalf.

It's rather foolish to invest the time and effort selecting top performers who can help you, then neglect to manage them around the objective of providing you the kind of business you want. Yet broker colleagues frequently tell me that they have buyer clients who don't follow the basics in maintaining good relationships. And as a result, they miss out on good opportunities.

Benefit of Being Straight Forward

"It's better not to let a broker know how much money you have. If you do, they're always trying to get you to use it all."

This is a rather common opinion which I've heard from a number of buyers. And my reaction is this: If you don't trust your broker, you need to either get a new one, or you need to adjust your ideas about how to work with someone who's trying to help you find a good business. Your broker or agent can't do a good job for you if he or she is not armed with all the relevant information about what you want and what you can do.

I remember being scolded by a client – a man who was looking for a non-retail business – because I didn't tell him about a convenience store located in his neighborhood that had come on the market.

He agreed that the business was well outside the parameters he had given me; Then said: "But I would have made an exception in this case."

Until brokers and agents develop the ability to read the minds of their clients, it's better for you, the buyer, to give your representative complete information about what you want, so that you don't miss an opportunity.

What business would you most like to buy? What is your second choice? Are there other types of enterprises you would consider if the circumstances were ideal? These are some of the questions to answer for yourself, and then discuss with the representative helping you to find a business. Also in the category of your requirements are topics such as how much money you need to earn and how many hours you want to work every week.

Your representative also needs to know, in as much detail as you can provide, about your capabilities: The sum of cash you have for a down payment and working capital, your tolerance for risk, your experience and skills, the level of debt you are willing to take on, the value of your real and personal property and the extent to which you are prepared to use it to collateralize any obligations you take on as part of a purchase.

Equipped with a good understanding about you as a potential buyer, the business sales professional will be able to help you and even will be motivated to work on your behalf. That's the payoff to you for being open and honest with your broker, and for providing all the information needed to serve you properly.

And a word of caution that buyers who aren't certain what they want in terms of the type of business, who aren't specific about the amount of cash they've got set aside for this purpose, and don't know – or won't reveal – how much real or personal property they're willing to put up as collateral in the event of seller financing, won't get a lot of broker attention. Business sales professionals have more than enough "customers" to stay busy. And so their focus will always remain with those buyers who show they are serious and committed by furnishing ample information about what they're looking for and what they can handle.

Maintain Good Communication

Just as it takes a good regimen with a nutritious diet and regular exercise to maintain your body in good shape, it requires maintenance – in the form of regular communication – to sustain a healthy relationship between a business buyer and his or her representative. A broker who doesn't hear from a client for awhile may conclude that the person has changed their requirements, or moved to another town.

If you've read an interesting article about franchises, send it to your representative. If you have questions about whether the changing economic climate has influenced the prices of small businesses, give your broker a phone call or send off an email. And if you're circumstances have changed – your cash reserves have grown or you're now willing to consider a good restaurant for sale although such a possibility was out of the question before – make sure your representative is one of the first people you tell. If nothing else, the steady stream of communication from you will force the broker to keep you in mind every time a new listing crosses the desk.

Considering that roughly half the buyers for small California businesses change their plans by taking a new job, becoming a partner or investor in an existing business with a friend or relative, or relocating out of the area, it would not be surprising if your broker or agent assumes you aren't serious and ready to make a purchase, and so, neglects to stay in touch with you.

How do you impress on him or her that you're not one of these people who will take up a broker's time finding out what's available, then will change their mind about buying a business? By communicating, that's how!

Call each representative at least once a week to say "hello" and to learn what is going on in the market. That reminder will separate you from the "tire kickers" (less serious buyers) and will help to keep your name at the top of the broker's list of people to call whenever an interesting and suitable business appears on the market.

Does this advice seem to be a matter of common sense? It is. And a surprising number of would-be buyers don't follow it. A typical sentiment was expressed by a buyer who told me: "I'm the customer. It should be the broker's job to stay in touch with me. Not the other way around."

This is a reasonable expectation in an ideal situation. But in the real world, most successful business sales professionals are – like most of us – very busy. They have more work to do than time to fit it all in. So they may not get around to calling everyone as often as they should.

Don't let this fact interfere with the good communications you maintain with your representative. The more he or she knows about what you need and can do, and the more they hear from you, the more likely that person will be to match you up with a business you like.

Reminder About Your Realistic Expectations

If you ask your broker or agent why some of the buyers don't get much of their help or support, you're likely to hear a complaint that they try, but never succeed, at pleasing over-demanding clients. And those are the clients who ultimately get the least consideration and attention.

A number of clients are only candidates for a business opportunity if it is priced below value, offered with unusually generous terms and is highly desirable in most every other respect. And since no business opportunity is perfect, these so-called buyers aren't likely to make a purchase. To an overworked business broker, people with unrealistic expectations are the ones to be contacted last, because they're bound to reject most anything proposed to them.

Everyone who's been looking in the market for awhile has heard of someone who bought a perfect business. I don't know if these are true stories or just business myths. But I encounter buyers who report things like: "There's a guy in Northern California who paid $50,000 for a business that earns $75,000 a year." Another story making the rounds is that a woman bought a retail store, for just the cost of inventory, and she is able to make $10,000 a month profit – and that's as an absentee owner.

I suspect these tales account for the fact that some people nurture their dreams of the perfect business. What they don't seem to realize is that they're just as likely to win a several million dollar jackpot in the California lottery as they are to be presented a business that meets their unrealistic expectations.

Instead, what you'll see, as you examine businesses for sale, are opportunities that have been priced a bit higher than their value (we'll get into how to determine the right price for a small California business in the next chapter), or that have a need for a cash infusion to upgrade equipment or increase the marketing activities, or are facing more aggressive competition from larger organizations in the same industry.

These businesses still are viable opportunities for the right buyer. But not for someone who wants the ideal company handed over on a silver platter. Indeed, unrealistic buyers are headed for disappointment. And they're unlikely to enjoy loyal cooperation from business brokers and agents.

Respect for Your Representative and the Protocol

To make sure that you maintain a working relationship with a broker who's trying to help you, it's important that you observe the simple requirements which insure efficiency and orderliness in the process of finding and buying a business.

Most people know it's not polite or productive to drop in, unannounced, on a business for sale, for the purpose of talking to the owner and employees. It's the job of the broker or the agent to set up an appointment for you to view the business and ask questions. But there are a few buyers who – becoming impatient with the process – want to make up their own rules. What they learn after embarrassing themselves, risking the confidentiality requested by the seller – and probably not gaining any more useful information than they would have obtained by working with the seller and broker – is that even if they want to buy the business, they will get little cooperation in doing so. That's not only the quickest way to alienate the business sales professionals, it also will turn the seller against the idea of cooperating with you.

And the subtle ways of violating the important confidentiality aspect of the procedure, are just as bad as the more obvious offenses. If you're bound to a non-disclosure pledge, you should understand that it applies wherever you happen to be, throughout your day, not just in the offices of the subject business.

A buyer I know of decided, while at a family picnic, to boast about the possibility of his acquiring a business for which he was negotiating. And he named the company, not realizing that an employee of that firm was in attendance at the event. In no time at all the word was out. The buyer had compromised the confidentiality he had agreed, in writing, to protect. And the end result was a lose-lose situation in that the seller and the broker were furious, and the buyer had lost the possibility of any cooperation from the business owner or from his (former) business broker.

Should You Pay a Broker or an Agent to Represent You?

Fortunately, most people understand and respect the necessity of complying with the simple requests from a broker; in return for the wealth of proprietary information they are provided. And some buyers have enough appreciation for the services they can receive from a competent broker or agent that when they meet one with whom they have a strong rapport, they wonder about hiring the person to represent them in the business buying process.

This is a matter that long has been debated. And there is no single and simple answer to whether you should hire a business sales professional to help you, thereby making the person your agent, and removing any possibility of a conflict.

Arguing in favor of this idea is the notion that someone who is clearly working on your side in negotiations will put all the effort into getting the price and terms you want. There will be no reservations about that, because as your representative, the broker has no contractual relationship with the seller.

Whether the arrangement is for you to provide a commission to your agent upon successful completion of a purchase, or to pay an hourly fee regardless of outcome, the lines of loyalty are clearly drawn. And if the person is able to get a better price and terms package than you could have obtained as your own negotiator, you'll recognize an immediate benefit from your decision to obtain the broker's services. This is also the case (that the broker will have justified the fee by gaining, for you, additional benefits of equivalent value) if your representative is able to help you get a low cost business loan to complete the purchase.

In other words, if you were to hire a business broker or agent to help you acquire a specific business, and promised to pay her $10,000 upon its successful purchase, you could say there is no cost to you for her services, if, for example, she is able to negotiate for an additional $10,000 worth of value (more than you could have) in the price and terms of the deal.

The other way of looking at this situation is that the representative whom you ask to write an offer on a business has a responsibility to you and, by law and custom, will be working on your behalf. "Accordingly," goes this argument, "there's no point in paying extra to someone for doing what they're supposed to do anyway."

I've spoken with buyers who line up on both sides of this issue – pro and con. The most recent opinion I heard on this matter was voiced by a man who bought a Southern California music store and said he was delighted to be able to get the business and that the fee paid to the buyer's broker who helped him was "well worth it."

Conclusion

In working with a business broker or agent in a campaign to find and purchase a suitable business, a buyer will have the best results by letting the representative know, in detail, what the buyer wants. And there is no benefit to holding back information and being less than candid with a representative trying to help.

Establishing and maintaining communication with a broker also is critical, as it keeps the representative motivated to notify you about suitable businesses for you to consider. But a buyer without realistic expectations about what can be acquired, and at what costs, will have a difficult time making good use of a business broker. They don't waste time with client prospects whom they are unlikely to be able to satisfy.

Buyers are reminded to observe the requirements of protocol when investigating possible business acquisitions. That includes respecting the non-disclosure/confidentiality agreement the buyer signs when told about an offering.

A discussion of the pros and cons of hiring a broker to represent you in finding and negotiating for a business demonstrates that buyers have differing ideas and approaches

KEY POINTS FROM THIS CHAPTER

❖ *For a business broker or agent to do a good job of finding you a suitable company to buy, he or she needs to know what you want, in as much detail as you can explain. It's difficult to provide service of this type to someone who is holding back vital information.*

❖ *And you increase the chances of having your representative let you know about every possible business for you, when you maintain an ongoing dialogue with the person – initiated by you, if needed.*

❖ *What can undermine your good relations with a broker is your requirement that a business you buy must be "perfect." Not only does it not exist, but your insistence that any offering proposed to you should have all positive factors and no flaws, will drive away brokers who might otherwise attempt to help you.*

❖ *Expectations about buying highly profitable businesses that is offered at a substantially discounted price are similar to the hopes that you'll win the California Lottery. Without realistic ideas about what is probably going to happen, people are not equipped to deal as well with the way things are.*

❖ *Although buyers know it's bad business to violate the Non-Disclosure/ Confidentiality agreement, some forget to honor their commitment. The results can be compromising the confidentiality requested by the seller, hurting the relationship between the seller and listing brokerage, and ruining the buyer's chances of purchasing that business or any other business through the brokerage.*

❖ *One benefit of paying a broker to help you find and purchase a small business is that there's no question about the representative's responsibilities – no conflict of interest.*

❖ *Some buyers argue that an able business broker or agent will "earn back" their fee by negotiating a lower price or better terms, or by arranging for low cost additional funding to help finance the purchase.*

❖ *The contrary argument is that the law and customary practices require a broker representing a buyer to work for that client's best interests; that there is no point in paying someone for services they're supposed to provide anyway.*

CHAPTER SEVEN

HOW MUCH SHOULD YOU PAY FOR A BUSINESS - 1?

As you evaluate possible business purchases, you probably will understand most aspects of each offering. The financial details will yield some of the operating information, and other facts will become clear when you review documents such as the equipment list and premises lease. But what's often difficult to comprehend about a small California business is its price.

Indeed, pricing a business for sale can be as much an art as a science. And because there is no single and definitive method for assigning an exact market value to a small business, many sellers feel justified in building plenty of negotiating room into their asking prices – usually too much room in my opinion.

There are various approaches to take when determining a business' correct selling price. The most important factor for you – the buyer – has little to do with knowing how to choose the right pricing formula. Instead it is determining if the business under study will generate enough money to do the following: Pay off any financial obligations with which you are burdened as part of the purchase, compensate you fairly for your labor in the company, and reimburse you for your capital invested. How quickly you expect that reimbursement to occur is a critical factor in establishing the correct price at which you want to buy the business.

Whether you are working with a broker or on your own, you ought to have a basic idea of the elements that go into pricing a small California business. For one thing, you'll want to know, when reviewing a business, if its asking price is realistic. And you'll want a method for doing some price calculations for yourself.

What Doesn't Work

To explain the difficulty inherent in assigning the "right" price to a small California business, it will be helpful to review a couple of approaches that have been tried and rejected as not quite applicable to the problem.

The familiar and time-honored comparables method gives home buyers and sellers, as well as real estate brokers, an easy and efficient way to figure out the right price for a two-story, three-bedroom brick house in a particular California neighborhood. The same principle applies for a two-bedroom bungalow, a 26-room mansion with servant's quarters, or most any other residential property for that matter. All you need to know are two things: The particulars of the subject property, and the sale prices recently recorded for similar houses in the area. Yes, there may be additions and subtractions to that number, in order to adjust for factors that aren't precisely comparable between the subject and related comparison samples. But these adjustments are part of the method that works to establish a home's value.

The key ingredient for the valuation formula – a database of recently sold comparable properties – does not exist in the business opportunities sector. No two businesses are even close to comparable. A small California business is a dynamic, changing entity that is shaped by the practices of management and employees. It takes on a unique personality based on the subtle influences of location and the makeup of the customer base.

Another idea that has been given consideration is the return on investment mechanism with which holders of corporate equities evaluate the contents of their portfolios. This approach addresses the question of how much income an investor receives in return for his or her capital. In this way it looks like the dynamics are the same as with the purchase of a small business. But the one substantial difference is that those who buy into the stock market play a purely passive role with respect to the companies in which they're invested. By contrast, anyone who's been in charge of a small business can tell you the owner's role is anything but passive.

The Market Approach

But we're on the right track. In fact, the solution is to combine the best features of the other methods into an approach which can predict with some accuracy, the sum that a buyer will pay for a small business and the seller will accept – in other words – the market value.

This method is applied by viewing completed transactions —this data is anecdotal, since there is no complete and thorough repository of information on "done" business deals as there is for real estate – and determining the relationship between the annual adjusted net income of a company and its selling price. So, for example, if small grocery stores in a particular part of California seem to be selling for a sum of approximately 2.5, times their annual adjusted net income, we can apply that multiple to other stores in that category and area. Their circumstances may be widely different: One may have brand new equipment; another, a particularly long lease, and these factors might influence the final figure. But by using the multiple of 2.5, and knowing the annual adjusted net income of a subject business, we can determine a figure that is approximately correct.

The multiple, expressed another way, is the expectation of annual adjusted net income from the business, as it relates to the amount of cash that was invested in purchase price and operating capital. In other words, the 2.5 multiple suggests that the buyers want their money back in two-and-a-half years.

The beauty of this solution is that it's not theoretical. It reflects the actual behavior in the market. And its weakness is that it's a general rule of thumb, subject to exceptions and disputes among interested parties.

Some business appraisers believe the price should include inventory, while others consider inventory to be in addition to the price. The right solution for this problem depends on a few factors, including the amount of inventory in relation to the value of other assets

In the give and take of the marketplace, a distribution or manufacturing business – a class of businesses much in demand – might bring a 3.0 or 3.5 multiple. For a business with problems – examples include a short term lease remaining, aging equipment and market encroachment by competitors – the correct multiple might be closer to 1.0 or 1.5. Retail businesses frequently fetch 2.5 to 3 times the annual adjusted net income if inventory is part of that price. The multiple might be a bit lower if it is not meant to include the inventory needed.

To arrive at the initial figure, we then need to determine annual adjusted net income. And this figure – also called "cash flow," or "seller's adjusted cash flow" – is calculated by adding the company's profit, with the stated income of the owner, and all business expense items which provide owner benefit. This last category includes health, auto and life insurance premiums paid by the company for the owner, the business' auto expenses and entertainment costs which are not needed to conduct operations, interest amount on notes paid by the business, depreciation and amortization above what's needed to replace capital equipment, and other items on the expense ledger that actually accrue to the benefit of the owner. (Please see the sample of the initial P&L and the adjusted P&L at the end of this chapter.)

Incidentally, it is this adjusted net income figure that is needed, rather than just the profits reported, in order to complete the computation. That's because each company has a different way of showing the distribution of income. Some small business owners, for example, choose not to show a profit, or they even show a loss, but take out large salaries and enjoy a number of company perks. The books for other enterprises might show a modest profit and modest salary for the owner. And in sole proprietorships, the reporting of company income is synonymous with owner's salary. For an accurate comparison, then, all these items are added together to arrive at the adjusted net income.

The easiest place to find the raw figures needed for the annual adjusted net income computation is in the year-end results for the most recently completed fiscal or calendar year. But if you can start with the most recently reported period – either the quarter or a past month – then calculate backward over a 12 month period, the resulting "annual" figure will reflect the most up-to-date performance of the business, and provide the most accurate conclusion. If, for example, the most recently reported activity is for the month of June, the analysis should include the 12 months going back through July for the previous year.

With this information – the annual net income of the subject business under scrutiny, and the multiplier common to transactions for this type of operation in your part of the state – you can calculate an initial figure that reflects a fair approximation of the company's market value.

This approach explains why the owner of a highly profitable airplane parts brokerage recently received a substantial price upon sale of his business, even though there were few assets included in the deal. And it is the same thinking that was behind the low offering prices for a manufacturing company with extensive equipment, but little adjusted net income. Other factors were considerations, but were largely outweighed by the matter of profitability.

Rather than convey the impression that this process is all very scientific – and the final price entirely predictable – I should make you aware that there's guesswork in both selection of a multiplier, and also the decisions about how much weight to give the various influencing factors.

Adjusting the Initial Figure

And in most cases there are factors that influence a company's value. They are accommodated with some fine tuning to the initial price that was determined using the multiple of annual adjusted net income method. Such factors as business location, terms of lease, extent of seller training, risk, future of the industry, ease of operating the business, and value of capital assets, all can have an impact on the value beyond the initial finding.

Clearly a great location and lease will enhance the appeal, and thereby boost the value of a retail business. So will a long history of earnings and a seller willing to stay on for an extended period to train the new owner – both factors that could reduce risk. And similarly, a business with a lease that soon will expire, and a downward trend in annual revenues over the past few years, will have to be offered at a discount – from what might otherwise be the initial price – in order for the owner to achieve a sale.

The requirement that a substantial sum of cash be added before a business can be operated correctly means the price should be adjusted accordingly. If a buyer needs to replace several pieces of equipment, for example, the investment will climb substantially beyond the down payment. This fact should be reflected in a lowered asking price to accommodate the circumstances.

Another powerful influence on the correct selling price for a small California business is the actual deal structure – the terms that go along with the price. This matter will be taken up in the chapter that follows.

And, of course, in the case of a distressed sale (for example, an owner/operator becomes ill and is unable to continue to run the business) the necessity of moving quickly can depress the price below the value which the business would bring under ordinary market conditions.

Market Realities

It was mentioned at the beginning of this chapter that many sellers ask a price for their businesses that is not supported by the circumstances. In other words, if a buyer analyzes the asking price of an offering in terms of annual adjusted net income, and the result is a multiple of 3.5, but the prevailing multiple in the market is 2.5 or 3.0 – with no other factors adding substantially to value – it's a safe bet that the seller wants to sell for more than the business is worth. This could be a bargaining ploy (with the idea of starting at a high price and negotiating from there), or the seller missed out on the California Lottery and figures he'll make up for it by getting a buyer that loves the business and doesn't know, or doesn't care that it's over priced.

If you like the business but not the price, you have a choice. One possibility is to make an offer at the price you believe it to be worth. Your proposal will have more impact if you or the broker (if a representative is involved) can explain to the seller how the offering price was reached. I've known this to work in some cases. The seller may say something like: "Well, I thought I'd try to get more, but if this is what it's worth, I'll agree to sell like that."

An offer that comes in under asking price also can aggravate a seller and result in no deal at all.

Another choice you can make is to decline to proceed on an over-priced offering unless and until the seller lowers the price. If your representative explains to the seller that you were interested, but not at the asking price, it may help to influence the seller to be more flexible. Or it could make him or her more resolute about getting the asking price or not selling at all.

I think there is only one tactic to pursue, however, if confronted with another market reality – the claim of unreported income.

"I show a $5,000 profit every month, but there's another $1,500 that I take out that I don't show on the books," is a typical statement from a seller who wants you to believe that there is more net income than is reflected in the records of the business – usually in an attempt to justify an asking price that is substantially above what would be fair.

By declining to proceed with this kind of an offering, you will save the time and energy that you may want to devote to finding good businesses for sale, rather than trying to uncover illusive – probably non-existent – extra profits, and dealing with someone whose honesty is in question. If there's some tax cheating going on with this business, what other schemes are being perpetrated under this company's name?

With the market valuation approach and a few ideas about other factors that influence value, you have some of the tools needed to determine the correct price for a business that may be of interest, and compare that figure to the actual asking price. To gain additional insight, please note in the following chapter how the deal structure can impact the price of a small California business.

Conclusion

While the pricing of a small California business is as much an art as a science, as evidenced by the fact that some sellers become "creative" when setting the asking price for their business, the preferred approach is a reliable way to predict what a willing buyer and seller will agree on – which is the definition of the "right" price. That approach uses a multiplier that is common to the type of business under scrutiny, and the adjusted annual net income reported for that business. The result of this formula is the initial figure, a starting place that can then be adjusted by other factors that increase or detract from the desirability of the business.

The other set of factors affecting price are contained in the deal structure. That topic is reviewed in the next chapter.

KEY POINTS FROM THIS CHAPTER

❖ *The most widely accepted approach for setting the "right" price of a small California business is a blend of the comparables method used to determine the value of residential real estate, and the ROI (return on investment) mechanism used to measure investments in corporate securities.*

❖ *To determine how much a small business is worth, it's necessary to learn the prices of businesses of its type, in relation to their annual adjusted net earnings. The result is the multiple, and that figure is then multiplied with the annual adjusted net earnings of the subject business. The total is the initial figure.*

❖ *Adjusted net earnings include profit, owner's salary, company perks to the ownership, non-cash expenses (such as depreciation), interest expenses and other "costs" for items not needed to conduct business.*

❖ *Determining the value of a home is made easy by the availability of all sales prices of completed transactions in a specific area and time period. No such resource is available for business sales. So the information needed to deter- mine a proper multiple for use in calculating a business' value is largely anecdotal and informally collected.*

❖ *Among the factors which can positively influence the price of a business are those which add to its desirability with, for example, a good lease, a long history of profitability, up-to-date equipment and the promise of extensive seller involvement.*

❖ *Examples of negative influences on value include a short-term lease and new competitors coming into the market.*

❖ *If a new owner is required to replace much of the company's equipment, or will have to make other expenditures to insure successful operation, the total amount of the investment – not just the down payment – should be used in calculating the value of the business.*

❖ *One market reality is that seller's often set an asking price that is higher than the value of the business. They hope to receive more than their company is worth and want to establish "negotiating room" with the idea they "can always come down."*

❖ *A buyer who likes a business that is over-priced can make an offer at a price which the buyer thinks is fair. Another choice is to decline to make an offer unless and until the price is lowered to a more market-realistic level.*

❖ *Another market reality is the claim by some sellers that the business receives additional income, but they don't report it. This idea is used to justify a price that is too high in relation to the company's reported adjusted net earnings. Buyers are advised not to rely on such statements – in fact to be skeptical about any statements made by a person who is not forthright in his or her business dealings.*

❖ *Also influencing selling price of a business is the overall deal structure. That's the subject of the following chapter.*

Phiquex Manufacturing

Profit and Loss FY 2004

Category	Item	$ Amount	%
INCOME			
	From operations	626,812.00	
	Other (consulting)	11,000.00	
	Returns/Allowances	486.00	
	Gross Revenues	**$637,326.00**	**1.00**
EXPENSES			
	Cost of Goods:		
	Labor	190,405.60	0.299
	Materials	81,577.72	0.128
	Total	271,983.32	.427
	Gross Profit	**$365,342.68**	
	Overhead:		
	Advertising/promotion	8,922.56	0.014
	Administrative	7,647.91	0.012
	Auto	5,735.93	0.009
	Bank Charges	637.32	0.001
	Depreciation/Ammort	10,834.54	0.017
	Health coverage	13,383.84	0.021
	Insurance	19,757.10	0.031
	Interest	10,197.21	0.016
	Janitorial	25,493.04	0.04
	Legal/Accounting	12,109.19	0.019
	Maintenance	7,010.58	0.011
	Miscellaneous	7,647.91	0.012
	Office/Computer	14,021.17	0.022
	Officer Salary	18,000.00	0.028
	Payroll services	4,461.28	0.007
	Rent	52,898.06	0.083
	Selling Expenses	12,746.52	0.02
	Shipping/Handling	17,207.80	0.027
	Supplies	11,471.88	0.018
	Travel	3,823.96	0.006
	Utilities	29,954.32	0.047
	Total Expenses	**$293,962.12**	**0.461**
Net Income		**$ 71,380.56**	**0.112**

Phlquex Manufacturing

Table of Add Backs to Compute Adjusted Net Income (Recast Financials)

Advertising/promotion	8,922.56	Sponsored Little League Team	1,200.00
Administrative	7,647.91	Sister's help running errands	3,250.00
Auto	5,735.93	Personal use est. 80%	4,589.00
Bank Charges	637.32		
Depreciation/Ammort	10,834.54	50% unneeded reserve	5,417.27
Health coverage	13,383.84	For officer and family	13,383.84
Insurance	19,757.10		
Interest	10,197.21		
Janitorial	25,493.04		
Legal/Accounting	12,109.19	Est. 25% for officer's personal	3,027.30
Maintenance	7,010.58		
Miscellaneous	7,647.91		
Office/Computer	14,021.17		
Officer Salary	18,000.00	Officer Salary	18,000.00
Payroll services	4,461.28		
Rent	52,898.06		
Selling Expenses	12,746.52	Personal Entertainment ($300/mo)	3,600.00
Shipping/Handling	17,207.80		
Supplies	11,471.88		
Travel	3,823.96	50% personal travel at trade show	1,912.00
Utilities	29,954.32		
Net Income	**$71,380.56**	**Total Add Backs**	**$54,379.41**
		Adjusted Net Income (Net Income + Total Add Backs)	**$125,759.97**

PLEASE NOTE THAT THIS INFORMATION REPRESENTS THE IDEAS OF THE SELLER AS TO WHAT CONSTITUTES ADJUSTED NET INCOME. BUYERS ARE URGED TO DISCUSS THIS ANALYSIS WITH THEIR ACCOUNTANTS AND TO DISCUSS WITH TAX ATTORNEYS THE TAX IMPLICATIONS REGARDING THE REPORTING OF INFORMATION.

THE SELLER DOES NOT REPRESENT THAT HE IS GIVING OUT, IN THE CONTEXT OF THIS INFORMATION, ANY ACCOUNTING OR TAX ADVICE.

CHAPTER EIGHT

HOW MUCH SHOULD YOU PAY - 2?

The art and science of setting the "right" price for a small California business begins as a simple multiplication problem. It uses a multiple that's representative from the type of business being analyzed, and the adjusted net income averaged over the past two to three years. Then it's necessary to adjust the initial result up or down to account for the influence of other factors – unique to that business – which impact price.

These ideas were explored in the previous chapter where it also was noted that the other component that contributes to pricing is the deal structure. And that's the subject of this chapter.

It's generally the case that a seller can get a higher price by offering to take it in the form of a down payment and a note for the balance. It follows logically that the reverse is also true – a high cash requirement can translate to a lower price.

Cash Requirements

For example, it is common for sellers who insist on an all-cash deal to receive roughly three-fourths of the sum that they might have gotten in a deal that offered a substantial amount of financing. The seller takes a hit for insisting on all cash not only because it's more difficult to find buyers willing and able to pay all cash – the more money needed, the smaller the population of prospective buyers – it also means the seller will walk away from the business with no further ties, once the deal is completed. And some buyers find that worrisome, preferring a seller to be motivated, for financial reasons, to see the company continue on successfully.

This concern about the seller's complete disconnection from the business can even increase the buyer's anxiety level, just as it would be increased by anticipating other factors that might raise the risks associated with the business. And as you learned in the previous chapter, the anticipation of increased risk is one of the forces that negatively influences the desirability of a business, and hence its selling price.

Owners seeking to maximize the proceeds from the sale of a small business, structure the financing with the request for a down payment that's 30% to 50% of the price and then they carry back the balance over an extended period – three to seven years is common – at a market rate of interest. This makes for an appealing package.

If you're considering a business which can be purchased this way, you'll appreciate the prospect of having a long time to pay for it. That makes it more affordable. And it's nice to know that the payments are coming out of the company's earnings, as if the business is paying for itself.

An opportunity in your price range is even more manageable, financially, if you'll have some of your cash left over after the down payment. It'll come in handy for working capital. And the seller's willingness to be your bank – to collect the price over a number of months or years after you take over – sends a positive message that the seller believes in the future of the business, and in you. That's so encouraging it might even persuade you to pay the seller's asking price, or at least increase your offer to a level that's a bit higher than you wanted to go. This is a common way in which terms impact price.

In the push and pull of negotiations over the price and payoff scheme for a small California business, it's clear that some flexibility on the part of either party can win them concessions in the price. More lenient terms offered by the seller often come packaged with the request that you meet the asking price. And if lowering the price is your most important negotiating consideration as the buyer, you might be able to argue for the reduction by emphasizing your willingness to put more than is asked into a down payment, or by agreeing to discharge the balance with substantial payments that clear it more quickly than the seller had anticipated.

Collateral

Another area in which you and the seller will negotiate – demonstrating flexibility or holding firm, depending on your needs and preferences – relates to how you will secure the debt owed to the seller. Your idea, most likely, is that the business itself should provide all the collateral required. In theory, if you failed at making regular payments, the seller could call the note due and assume ownership of the business – either to operate or to sell off its assets.

The seller, however, may have different security in mind, such as a second trust deed in your home. The reasoning is that if you were to default on the obligation, that probably would mean the business was failing, and there may not be enough value remaining to equal your outstanding debt to the owner. Consequently, sellers frequently seek other security.

Again, there's a strong relationship between price and terms. The seller's willingness to accept a more buyer-friendly plan for securing the loan may be offered in exchange for your willingness to go along with a selling price you consider to be on the high side.

This agreement, seen from another perspective, suggests that the higher price enjoyed by the seller can come with a heightened risk for the seller, namely that in the event of your default on the loan, there may not be enough collateral to enable the seller to recover the total amount due.

To a great extent these relationships between price of a business offering and the terms, are entirely understandable. The opposing desires, modified with compromises made to achieve a mutually-sought outcome, give both the buyer and seller a chance to contribute to the final agreement. The price is indeed affected by the terms. But by how much? What can the prospective buyer take away from this as a guide used for equating price with other components of a deal?

Without a database of completed deals that we can research to analyze the details of each transaction, there probably is no practical way to discover repeated patterns, and then draw precise conclusions about the relationship between price and deal structure involved in the sale of a small California businesses. The many decisions that bring a buyer to the conclusion for or against a particular business, and at a specific price based on the terms, are   reached with both objective analysis – using the methods discussed in the previous chapter – and subjective process. That's why I consider the pricing of a small business by a seller, and the decision – on the buyer's part – about what that business is worth, to be the work of both art and science.

Do the Math

Whether or not the combination of price and terms for a particular small business is "right" can be determined on a calculator in a few minutes. Will the adjusted net earnings support the buyer working in the business, and also support the debt service which the buyer shouldered in order to purchase the business? If so, it's an indication the price and terms are right. If not, it's likely that the buyer's purchase was done at the wrong price and terms, in which event the buyer may face trouble ahead.

The simple calculation that determines if a business deal makes sense applies to the most elementary deal structure as well as to more complex sales arrangements. It is the ultimate test that buyers must use, even when the details of their transactions are configured in different, rather unusual ways to accommodate special needs. Some examples of creative deals will be useful:

EarnOut

The owner of a greeting card and gift shop in Southern California was undecided about whether to sell her business and retire. She really felt she needed to cut back on her work and take life easier. But the area near downtown where she'd had the business for years was experiencing resurgence. Finally! Large office buildings were being built, more people were coming to the neighborhood and sales at the shop were beginning to climb. If the selling price was related to business performance, she felt that hanging on another year, and showing a strong 12 months of sales and profits, would translate to a much higher price. And she believed she deserved the highest price she could collect after her years of hard work and meager profits when the area had been in decline.

The deal she worked out with an interested buyer was designed to let her retire right away, and also allow her to share in the bounty to come. Along with the down payment she received a promissory note from the buyer with its ultimate value determined by sales revenues collected by the business. The initial amount of the note was $35,000, and it was agreed that the value of the note would be increased by the same rate as the increase in business in the first year of operation by the buyer, compared to the previous 12-month period. So, for example, if sales doubled during the 12 months following close of escrow, compared to the previous 12 months, the value of the note would increase to $70,000 and the payments needed to amortize this balance would jump substantially. It was a good deal for both parties. And when the buyer did the analysis, he realized that with a higher level of business he could support the larger obligation as readily as he was able to make payments on the $35,000 note from the lower income stream.

The conclusion we can draw from this is that the underlying logic still worked – the income was sufficient to support the obligation – even though the structure of the transaction was different from most deals.

A reverse earnout might be an appropriate remedy in the event there is a possibility of some future occurrence that would seriously impact the profitability of the business in a negative way. Suppose, for example, there are rumors that a large competitor may be coming to the area in a couple of years. The buyer would insist on a much lower price because of the risk that this would damage business, but the seller would feel that if he agreed to the discount, and then the feared event never occurred, the buyer would be getting a deal that was too good.

The solution might be to structure a promissory note that can decline by the same rate as the drop off in business, if that were to happen. The $100,000 note might become a $66,666 note if gross sales were reduced by one-third, as a result of the arrival of the competitor. The note adjustment plan would assure the buyer of having a reduction in payments to the seller if gross sales are negatively affected as a consequence of this anticipated problem.

Incorporating an adjustable note into the deal structure is, in effect, allowing for a price change based on events in the future. It's a very clever way to make sure the price accurately reflects conditions of the business if either a windfall or a negative event is anticipated for the company. But to be effective, the agreement should contain clear definitions and terms that are spelled out in detail. Otherwise, there is a danger that a misunderstanding and distrust will undermine the intent of the agreement. In the case of the second scenario, if there was a decline in business – but it was due to the buyer's mismanagement and not due to injurious competition – an argument would follow. Parties might even have to go to court if the buyer requested that the note amount be reduced.

Delayed and Balloon Payments

And how can a seller accommodate a buyer who has put all of his or her capital into the down payment and is worried about having enough funds left over for working capital? One solution is for the seller to structure the promissory note so the payments don't begin until 90 days, or even six months following close of escrow. That way, the buyer has a bit of breathing room, and can build cash flow instead of making payments on the note for the first few months.

Another innovative approach uses balloon payments due later in the life of the note, instead of monthly payments that have to be paid from the beginning. This strategy can help a buyer through the first few months when available cash is critical for success. It works best, of course, if it is anticipated that business income in subsequent months will be sufficient to fund a reserve that is earmarked for paying the balloon.

Creative agreements also can resolve problems that crop up during negotiations over the issue of collateral. A seller might understandably want real estate security for a promissory note, if the note's value exceeds the amount that could be raised by selling the business' hard assets (if that should become necessary). And yet the buyer's objection that the business should represent the security for the obligation also is understandable. In fact, the buyer could argue that if the seller thinks the business isn't worth what the buyer will owe on it, after making a down payment, maybe the business is priced too high.

One solution is for the buyer to issue two notes with a total value equal to the amount the seller is carrying back. The first note would be secured by the business; the second note would be smaller, and secured by real property. In the event that the seller had to foreclose, both assets would be available, but there would be a limit to the amount the seller could recover from the buyer's property.

Each of these examples demonstrates a way that the price paid for a business, or the terms by which it is paid, can be altered to reflect the particular circumstances involving the transaction, the principals and the business. As long as the buyer and seller want to have a deal, and are willing to be creative and flexible, there is almost no obstacle that can't be overcome. But their ideas have got to be grounded in reality. And the math has to work.

No matter how ingenious the deal structure may be, if proceeds from operation of the business won't do what the buyer expected – usually that means, at minimum, supporting the cost of the acquisition – the transaction doesn't make sense. Eventually the buyer, and probably the seller also, will suffer the results of their bad planning. The buyer stands to lose his or her investment as well as the business; the seller won't collect the full purchase price bargained for, and may end up in court, battling to keep what was collected.

Conclusion

To complete the discussion about the factors involved in setting the price on a small California business – in order to help a buyer to understand whether a particular business seems to be fairly valued – the influence of deal structure needs to be considered. Deal structure includes the amount of cash down payment required as a percentage of the price, and the terms of seller financing, which is the note or notes which the seller is willing to receive for the difference between the price and the down payment. There are a number of ways to arrange seller financing to accommodate the particular needs of the buyer. But these strategies don't occur in a vacuum. They often work together with a modification in price to make sure the entire package works for the buyer, so that he or she will be able to pay off the seller.

KEY POINTS FROM THIS CHAPTER

❖ *Influencing the "correct" price of a small California business is the structure of the deal by which the sale is achieved.*

❖ *An all cash requirement on the part of the seller can mean that he or she will have to offer a discount of up to 25% off the asking price to achieve an agreement. This is because only some buyers will agree to put all cash into a deal.*

❖ *One reason that buyers are reluctant to pay the price all in cash to a seller, is that if the buyer runs into a problem with the business and could use some assistance from the seller, that aid is not likely to be provided; the seller is completely out of the deal and has no motivation to cooperate.*

❖ *An attractive deal structure involves a down payment of 30% to 50%, and a three to seven-year period to pay off the seller at a market rate of interest in monthly installments.*

❖ *Variations on this program can include an "earnout" or "reverse earnout," in which the value of the note may change, due to specific circumstances impacting the business. It's important that if principles are using a particularly creative deal structure, all the terms need to be thoroughly discussed and clearly laid out in the contract.*

❖ *Willingness of the seller to help you by financing part of the purchase price raises the perceived value of that business – if only because the seller's message is that he or she trusts you will do well enough, at least, to meet your obligations.*

❖ *If there is a difference of opinion between a buyer and seller as to what collateral should be used to secure the buyer's obligation, one solution is to include two notes, one secured by the business and the other, a smaller note, secured by the buyer's real estate.*

❖ *Regardless of how creative a deal, it still has to work when the buyer does the math. Will it pay for the buyer's labor as well as support the debt service incurred to purchase it?*

CHAPTER NINE

SMART SEARCH PRACTICES

In the event you thought the purchase of a small California business is much like any other purchase, with eager sellers vying for your attention and your dollars, you're in for a major surprise. As difficult as it is to buy a home in many of the hot California real estate markets, the acquisition of a business is even more of a challenge.

It's not just the possibility of having to compete with other buyers that makes it difficult to become the owner of an existing fast food franchise, or a small plastic forming company, or whatever business you've been considering. You'll find yourself embarked on a grand campaign – a frustrating one at times – as you consider all of the offerings, rejecting the vast majority of them, and keeping alive that hope of finding one that you like and that meets your criteria.

Patience is a Key Requirement

As was noted in an earlier chapter, the work of finding a suitable business can take 6 months in the best case and more frequently, up to 2 years. Maybe even longer. So it might be a good idea for you to hang on to your day job – at least for now.

Many small business owners are unrealistic or uninformed – perhaps both – when they decide to sell. They manage to crowd the market with offerings that aren't well prepared to be offered to buyers. And that means you, the buyer, will be asked to look at companies with serious problems (short time remaining on the lease, a history of financial losses, a high level of uncollected receivables), and very high asking prices.

Considering that only three in ten small businesses are sold, chances are that less than one-third of the offerings presented to you might seem to have the essentials needed to be desirable to any potential buyer. And of those, only a few will represent the kind of business you want; and fewer still will meet your financial requirements.

And if, after looking at hundreds of prospective businesses, you identify a few to investigate further, you'll then discover only a handful of this much smaller population to be worth making an offer on.

That's when you'll move into the next phase of your search, this time, competing with other buyers for the few sensible offerings in your area of interest and financial needs.

A Little Discipline

If you've played baseball or softball, you'll understand the analogy between looking for a suitable business to buy and waiting for a pitch to come right over home plate in the middle of the strike zone. The relevant advice here is not to try to buy something out of frustration and impatience, just as the pitching coach will tell you to resist the urge to swing at anything just because you've waited in the batter's box so long and you're eager to get a hit.

Like a curve ball coming at you, a business you're considering may not be what it seems. In fact, in most cases it is not what you thought when you first learned about it.

Talking to buyers and prospective buyers is revealing for all the stories they tell about the weeks and months of meetings with prospective sellers and with business sales professionals. One buyer who finally found a distribution business he liked after more than two years of a continuous search, explains that the hardest part was forcing himself to continue looking at possibilities, knowing that each was almost certainly going to be a waste of his time. But he did it anyway and stayed on his mission.

He explains that he changed his optimistic mindset: "I finally got out of the habit of thinking 'maybe the next business opportunity I hear about will be the one for me.' I got to the point – when I'd go to see a business or meet with a broker about something – that I knew for sure I was not going to like what they had to show me.' It helped me to not be so disappointed."

Be Ready to Move

Now that the buyer is in a properly cautious frame of mind, is convinced that most every business reviewed will be inappropriate, and is afraid to "take a swing" at an offering that seems to be interesting but may turn out to be a "curve ball," I should point out that you'll never buy a business if you are one of those "buyers" who become too cynical or fearful to ever make a bid. You've got to make an offer on what looks appealing.

Many buyers let the horror stories about over-priced listings and buying mistakes deter them from making a move on a business opportunity, even if they like it. After repeatedly examining companies for sale that were revealed to be unsatisfactory, a buyer might (understandably) conclude that every business which seems, at first glance, to be interesting, has a fatal flaw. It's just a matter of discovering what the problem is.

But if a business stands up to the initial investigation: If the revenues appear to be there, the reputation is sound, the future seems promising, the premises pass inspection and the price and terms appear within reason, it's imperative that you put in your purchase proposal.

82

Remember that you still can refuse to move forward on the transaction if your due diligence reveals problems with the company that you didn't see at first.

You may not get to see very many good businesses that meet your criteria, but if you look long enough, you will see a few. When it appears you've discovered that unique situation, don't neglect to put in an offer to buy it.

Selling Yourself to the Seller

An interesting finding that I've repeatedly confirmed in my conversations with sellers over the years is that even though their main priority, initially, was to get the most money possible under the best terms, at least half admit their final decisions had more to do with the quality of the buyer than the size of the deal.

The factor that persuaded many to enter into a deal, even at a price and terms less than they were asking, was simply that they liked the buyer and felt the person would be successful in the business.

As noted in the previous chapter, the buyer's success in the business directly impacts the seller, particularly when there is seller financing involved. And there may also be a psychological reason to explain why sellers sometimes – incredibly – put personality ahead of profits. The buyer who respects what the seller has accomplished with the business, and who shows enthusiasm for the ideas and systems the seller has put in place over the years, will probably make that seller feel pretty good about himself or herself. And that feeling is quite likely to help the seller become favorably disposed to the buyer's bid to purchase the business.

I'm not advocating that you pour so much praise on the other person that they need to "get out the shovel" but that you acknowledge the good work the seller has accomplished – after all, this is one of the few businesses you might want! And make it clear that you are open to the seller's ideas for insuring the company's continued success.

As is often the case, yours might be one of two, or even of three proposals being considered by the seller. If you are the seller's favorite prospect, it will help decide in your favor, in the event other offers are close to yours in price and terms. And even if your bid is too low, the seller may want to counter offer your proposal with the price at which he or she is willing to sell, and give you the option of getting first in line to buy by saying yes to the counter offer.

Part of that respect for the seller is demonstrated by recognizing and observing the conditions of showing that the seller has requested. I hear of too many instances where a buyer violates the non-disclosure and privacy pact to which he or she agrees as a condition of learning about a business. It is not all right to discuss the business owners' intention to sell with employees, vendors, customers, or with anyone else for that matter. Even if the seller claims to have revealed the truth about the sale, it is not the buyer's job to let the information out. That's up to the seller.

Even with an accepted offer that's going into escrow, unless you have the express permission of the business owner to take it up with certain parties (such as the company's vendors and customers), there is no justification for you to discuss the impending sale with anyone except your advisors. Violating the non-disclosure requirement is probably the quickest way to alienate the seller and lose the deal. And that might not be all your worries if the seller wants to hold you liable for some loss suffered because of what you said to whom.

Conclusion

Smart search practices include being patient, as it may take from 6 months to 2 years before you find the "right" business, and being disciplined, so you don't run out of patience and buy a company that is not right, just because you feared having no business to show for your many months of trying to find one. The buyer is encouraged, though, not to err in the other direction. So when you discover a business that *does* seem right, your best move is to make an offer. Even if it doesn't meet the seller's requirements, if you get a counter offer, at least you've got things moving forward on a company you think you'd like to own. You also are advised to sell yourself to the seller, beginning with the day of your first meeting. This can help to persuade the other party to work with you if you want to buy their business.

KEY POINTS FROM THIS CHAPTER

❖ *Considering that only 3 out of 10 small businesses on the market ever sell, it's most likely that the majority of opportunities you'll be exposed to are not in a condition to be marketable. From that short list of possibilities, you'll reject most offerings, as they will not be of interest to you, or not in your price range.*

❖ *It's necessary for a person wanting to purchase a small California business to be very patient. Your hunt will go on for a long time and may subject you to a number of hopeful moments – when you think you've discovered a suitable business – that change into times of disappointment, when you discover a business is not as appealing as it first seemed.*

❖ *Another search practice to adopt is one of discipline. I've seen buyers become so frustrated at the long months of effort with no results that they finally purchase a business that is not what they want, just so they can get on with managing a company and put an end to the "business shopping."*

❖ *It's not uncommon to be frustrated in the search, particularly when you see businesses you like, only to learn they aren't as profitable as you'd thought, and will require more working capital than you'd anticipated.*

❖ *Another frustration comes about when a buyer finally discovers a suitable business, only to lose out to someone else who saw it first, or who offered the seller a better deal.*

❖ *Selling yourself to the seller is an important and useful strategy if you want your offer to be carefully considered and if you want to look forward to his or her cooperation throughout the negotiating process and beyond.*

❖ *Your observance of the non-disclosure agreement will help you maintain a solid relationship with the seller and keep you out of trouble.*

CHAPTER TEN

A LITTLE PLANNING GOES A LONG WAY

Anna was determined to provide for her five children. She was their only parent, ever since that night when government troops stormed into the little house where they lived in their native county, and hauled her husband away, probably to be shot to death or locked in prison for life. Her plan to operate a grocery store in San Francisco, once they could come to the U.S., had the advantage that with her hard work, she could earn enough money to take care of her family. And the store would provide a good environment for the children to learn about business and to form good work habits during after school hours and on weekends, when they helped out by stocking shelves, cleaning the coolers and floors and – for the oldest ones – taking shifts at the cash register.

Also, she would meet others in the business community and would be a helpful resource for relatives – some of whom had contributed to the fund she had raised to help in purchasing the business – who would be coming to this country seeking employment, or a business to buy.

Anna got a job at a busy convenience store so she could begin earning money and learning the business, and she investigated offers of businesses for sale. Unfortunately, though there were several on the market that seemed suitable, they all required more cash than she had. The smaller ones, that she could afford, did not produce the income she needed for her family.

Not one to give up, Anna made a few offers that called for more seller financing – that is, less down payment – than was requested by the sellers. None of these was accepted.

What to do?

Anna then explored the possibility of borrowing additional funds from institutions that were guaranteed repayment by a Federal government program managed through the SBA (Small Business Administration). She qualified as to need and she satisfied the government requirements for experience with the business, particularly after being rewarded by her employer with promotion to shift manager.

She was stumped, however, by the prospective lender's requirement that she provide a business plan. She'd never prepared a business plan – never had even seen one – and wasn't quite clear why they were asking that of her.

An officer of the bank explained that they weren't interested in her writing skills – she still was learning to express herself in English – and they didn't expect her to demonstrate the knowledge or ability of a business school graduate. They wanted her to go through the exercise so that she would be forced to think about setting goals for her business and would give some thought as to what might be required to achieve those goals. In other words, they wanted to get her in the habit of planning – anticipating the problems and opportunities which might be encountered by the business, and then deciding what to do to avoid or minimize the problems and to take full advantage of the opportunities. In short, they wanted to know that if they leant the money to help her purchase the business, she would know what to do once the business was hers. If so, they had a good chance of being repaid.

What a great idea!

Imagine the benefits to our businesses, maybe even our economy, if every owner of a small California business – any business anywhere, for that matter – were to consider the question of what to expect in their area and in their industry, and then considered strategies for dealing with those anticipated factors.

That's the essence of planning and I strongly recommend that once you find a business you like, you spend some time thinking about it, the markets it serves, the characteristics that make it unique, and the problems that might be encountered. Then develop a plan that will maximize its strengths and address its challenges.

Why You Should Write a Business Plan

This book is not about business planning. It's about finding a suitable business to buy, determining how much it is worth to you, and structuring a deal that works for you and for the seller so that you can complete a purchase. But I think that if you can conduct a little business planning as part of that endeavor, it will increase your chances of being successful.

The ability to prepare a business plan will help you persuade a lender that you are a worthy recipient for a loan, and it will possibly become a valuable tool for you in running your business – developing a vision for your enterprise and translating that vision into practical programs that will contribute to your company's success. And when it comes time for YOU to sell, your business planning know-how may help maximize the value of what you show to buyers, which translates into the highest price for your offering.

The planning discipline

If you would like to distinguish yourself in business and set your company apart from most others in your area and in your industry, the one simple thing you can do is to adopt the discipline of formal, systematic and regular planning. To tell yourself: "I'll swing by the post office and pick up some stamps on my way to the cleaners, because it's on the way...." is a form of planning, but it's the last-minute, haphazard kind, not formal and systematic. Unfortunately, most business planning is of this last-minute kind.

You probably recognize the value of the organized and long-term planning to which I refer. Chances are, however, that once you're engaged in the many tasks and subject to the pressures of running your own business, you'll find it nearly impossible to set aside uninterrupted time, escape the daily demands, and clear your mind of the most recent emergency so you can focus on the "big picture."

I frequently observe the frustration experienced by business owners who are so overwhelmed with the pressing matters requiring their immediate attention that they feel it's a luxury to plan out a single day – never mind developing a long-range strategy for their companies.

And I've heard all the arguments from those who feel that just-in-time responding is more appropriate than planning for today's fast moving, rapidly changing business environment. Besides, I know some business people feel that to plan is to foster a kind of rigid thinking and inflexibility in response to problems and opportunities, that are contrary to an organization's best interests.

My observations, however, convince me that proper planning can aid in the effort to keep a company moving forward toward specific objectives, without sacrificing the "dexterity" necessary for survival in the contemporary business environment.

The planning benefit

As noted above, planning is a "simple" solution that can be applied to the problem of enabling your future company to be successful in its marketplace. But just because it's a "simple" solution for a number of business challenges does not make it "easy" to implement. And that's why so many business people acknowledge the importance of preparation but neglect to practice it in any consistent or meaningful way.

What they are missing by not doing their planning is the benefit of referring to a set of worthwhile goals – arrived at after careful thought – and a blueprint for achieving those goals. Also being missed is the "way of thinking" that is developed as a byproduct of the planning process, and is associated with people who run organizations that are successful.

What's meant by "way of thinking?"

I know a manager of an auto dealership who works 12 and 14-hour days, usually seven days a week (leaving him little time to spend with family), focused mostly on dealing with the problems that come up, one right after the other, every day in the business. He's constantly pulled from one company department to another, solving customer complaints and employee problems, responding to demands from the manufacturer that supplies cars, the banks which provide financing, and the members of the community who object to the noise and auto traffic generated by his business. Meanwhile, it's a full time job just keeping operating costs from getting out of hand. Ask him to describe the company and he'll discuss the various challenges that pop up each day, and the tiring work required to meet them. His mind is always on the latest problems. He is working hard trying to manage this chaos, and it is from this experience that he forms his way of thinking.

Another dealership with which I'm familiar is run by a person I call a "leader" rather than a manager. His firm has the same problems just mentioned, but they are handled by his subordinates, following proscribed procedures in which they have been trained. He has defined the company in terms of two specific objectives – the commitment to high customer satisfaction and the consistent effort to increase sales and profits. These themes are evident in the posters on the walls and in the newsletters circulated to all employees. And they are reinforced with an incentives program that rewards employees (he calls them "team members") for good ideas and special efforts that help the company meets its objectives. Much of this person's time is spent interacting on the golf course or over lunch with community leaders and executives of local companies which purchase or lease cars in fleet quantity. This is someone who rarely deals with the day-to-day problems of the dealership, although he receives regular reports informing him of everything going on in the company. He considers his job mostly fun, and he is careful not to let it intrude on his personal life. His is an entirely different "way of thinking" than that of the manager from the dealership first mentioned.

Oh, and I should note that the second company is much more successful than the first: It makes more money, has more satisfied customers and happier employees.

The difference between the style of these two managers, and is plain to see, has to do with the way each "thinks" about his job and how to best accomplish it.

The reader is encouraged to gain from these ideas the concept that if you will take the time and put forward the effort to think about your business, by imagining how it could be most productive and easy to operate, then get to work on tactics to actually realize that vision – or come as close as you can, the very process of doing this exercise – of preparing a plan for your business – will help you adopt a way of thinking that will lead to success for you and your company.

Your Planning Skills

In discussing the ideas about preparing business plans with owners of small California businesses, I notice that some people are intimidated and a little unnerved. They don't feel competent to develop a plan, and they aren't sure about their writing skills, particularly if the plan needs to be done in English, which may not be the business person's first language. Don't worry. You need not be a great thinker, a terrific writer or even a first rate business problem solver. The skill is one that develops over time, as you stay with it and continue to learn how to do it. In fact, by preparing such a plan, say once a year, for your business, and modifying it every few months in between, you will notice that you will continue learning more about general business topics, about your specific industry and geographic area,

And you needn't have all the answers as you learn to tap sources, such as the SBA (U.S. Small Business Administration), your chamber of commerce and perhaps convention and visitors' bureau, and the business section of your public library. You will notice that you are sharpening your investigative skills and finding more and more places to get the information you need to develop informed and useful plans.

Elements of Your Plan

There probably are dozens of formats for a business plan, organized in a variety of different ways, depending on the intended function – whether for funding, for a company's internal use, or another purpose. Business schools, business book publishers and business consulting services all have their own approach to the issue of planning for a business to deal with the challenges, and the exploit the opportunities likely to be encountered in the near and long-range future. But most forms follow the same general outline and include these components:

Objective

The statement of the goal set for the business is usually at the beginning of the plan. It focuses on the purpose for the planning. And it should include a definitive description of what is intended. This section usually does not get the attention it deserves, which is why we see business plans with objectives that are vague and general. The foundation of a good plan is a clearly defined objective that is achievable – but not without work and application of good ideas – and worth accomplishing. And a proper objective should be measurable, with a time element incorporated.

I've seen too many business plans built around weak objectives and it makes one wonder if the entire plan is simply an empty exercise. To "increase sales" is too general and an objective of "make business better" begs the "why" question. In other words, who will benefit and how will they benefit if business is better? Also, there are no clues in this objective about how the "increase" goal will be measured, nor do we know if this is a plan that is to take place over the next six weeks or six years, at which time, presumably, the objective will have been achieved.

A lender or other professional viewing your business plan wants to see a real, optimistic but not overly aggressive objective stated something like this: "Increase sales for XYZ Company in the 12 month period from January 2005 through December 2005, by ten percent compared to sales achieved in the same 12-month period in 2004." The logical and specific thinking that goes into formulating an objective like this, will probably lead to a plan that is understandable, realistic and can be acted upon. And that's the way to achieve your stated objective.

Background

Explain some basics about the company. Include a short history, noting length of time in business, type of product or service provided, a general description of the clientele, a few words about the premises, its location and terms of the lease or statement of the fact that the property is owned by the business owner. And a quick rundown on the employees belongs here – how many and what is the composition of the staff – (skilled, unskilled, full-time, part-time, union or non-union members?)

Some information about the company's financial situation might go next. Most plans include operating statements – balance sheets and P&Ls going back five years – as an exhibit placed at the end of the regular document. But it might be useful to include a brief summary of the numbers early in the plan, as part of the general description of the company. This is particularly important for a plan that will be used in an effort to persuade a lender to provide you financing to buy or to expand a business.

Other pertinent facts regarding the company should also be noted. What is unique or unusual about it? Has it enjoyed any special privileges (if writing about Haliburton, for example, you might want to note that the former CEO is now Vice President of the United States with a lot of opportunity to influence military spending by the Federal government), or does it have a particular vexing difficulty to overcome (think of mobile home builders in the Southeastern part of the U.S. subject to regular destruction of their facilities during hurricane season).

External circumstances

Once the company is introduced, the next step in the development of the business plan is to review the environment in which it conducts business and let the reader know what challenges are posed by these external circumstances, and what particular opportunities might be presented. Some of the questions that should be addressed are: How big is the market for the company's products or services? Is the market growing or shrinking? What do customers want? How are customer habits, tastes, economic or lifestyle issues changing what they want as it relates to what you provide? Has the competitive picture changed, or do you expect it to do so in the future? How is the local economy and how might it change in the months and years ahead? How much is your industry affected by economic conditions?

Other comments to include about the external world in which your company functions have more to do with non-marketing issues, such as government regulations and environmental concerns, and the status of the employee pool, if your company is in a labor-intensive business.

What you are getting at, in the description of the external circumstances, has to do with their influence on your likelihood of meeting your objective for the business. A growing market for what you offer may nicely fit with your objective, enabling you to enjoy the 10 percent growth without doing anything that's new or different. But your analysis of the environment in which you function will probably reveal some factors which could prevent or limit growth, and hinder your company's progress toward the objective. What will you do about these problems? Your planning should include the strategies you intend to employ in order to overcome these challenges that are external to your company.

Are more competitors expected to participate in your market? If so, you'll need to determine if you can lower prices or improve service in order to maintain an edge over the competition, so as to retain current customers and gain even more. Maybe the solution is to promote business more aggressively or differently. And if you recognize the possibility of a shortage of the capable labor you'll need to meet your objectives, the ideas in your plan might include recruiting for new employees at trade schools where relevant skills are taught, advertising job openings in other parts of the country or of the state where there may be qualified workers who would like to relocate to your area. Or, perhaps it makes sense to offer an unusually attractive employment package with incentives to lure qualified employees to your company.

Every factor and all circumstances likely to impact the company's ability to meet the objective should be noted, along with your ideas for dealing with the challenges.

And don't despair if you can't immediately come up with a solution for every problem. The fact that you're aware of the possible difficulties and are giving them some thought and consideration probably puts you ahead of most of your competitors. As noted above, the majority of business owners – and that includes companies fighting for your customers – are struggling to meet customer demands, cover for sick employees, and deal with other urgent problems. They'd like to plan ahead and prepare for future circumstances, but usually can't find the time and energy. Your ability to actually focus on the future, to develop a concrete vision for your organization in the months and years from now, and to begin implementing procedures meant to help the company meet somewhat ambitions objectives, may enable your organization to thrive while others continue to struggle.

Start by understanding the issues you face, even if the effective solutions you need aren't popping up right away. They are likely to come to you as you ponder the problems and research the various resources available to help. That includes getting a little education – formal or informal – about others in your position, with similar problems, and how they were able to overcome their obstacles.

Your analysis of external circumstances also may reveal opportunities that ought to be exploited in order to move you toward meeting your objective. I recently heard a business owner talk about the new housing development full of potential customers who should be informed about his organization's services. And the reader probably hears the same type of conversation from a manager who may say, for example, "We keep getting requests for that new item. We probably should get it in stock, but I don't have time to research how to do that."

If, in fact, these ideas would increase business and profitability, the owners who know about these things and don't do anything to make them happen, are not doing a competent job of running their organizations. The heart of the strategy for taking advantage of an opportunity might involve simply finding the time to embrace that opportunity, taking advantage of it, for the benefit of the company.

Factors internal to the organization

After a review of what's going on outside the company – the things you can't change, but you can prepare for and adapt to – it's time to look inside your organization and determine the shape of the systems, procedures and circumstances over which you do have control.

Are there employees not carrying their weight? Does the costly rent cover a space that is too big for your needs? Do you suspect you are spending too much in the way of the company's resources on business sectors that are not profitable, while neglecting markets and services that would bring in much more income?

These are factors that can and should be changed. And like some of the external problems, these circumstances represent obstacles which you need to determine how to remove, or get around, so that you can meet those objectives you've set for your business. The hard part in making internal changes, incidentally, may simply be getting the courage to do what needs to be done. There's no reason you have to tolerate an incompetent employee. But you need to have the guts to deliver him the "pink slip."

And if aging machinery is making it difficult for you and your employees to productively provide your firm's services, you need to bite the bullet and face that problem, prepared to do whatever you need to do in order to fix it. It may mean loading the firm with new debt or violating your long-standing principle that calls for purchasing, rather than leasing the capital equipment used in your business.

Indeed, you can change most of the internal factors that make your organization stumble on the path toward achieving the objectives you've established. You can do it. And I've noticed that in many organizations at which troubling internal circumstances seem to persist, the real stumbling block is usually the owner's reluctance to make changes.

As you describe, in your business plan, the internal circumstances that might work against the achievement of your objective, it's probably time to outline the solution you see to these problems. If you're more likely to pursue the solution by breaking it down into small, incremental actions – making it seem less daunting and more manageable – just list those steps in your plan. That's what plans are for: To lay out a blueprint of a solution for a problem.

And like the effort to deal with external factors, you'll find there are resources you can call on to help manage the internal issues that need to be resolved.

Using Your Business Plan

The most obvious practical purpose for your business plan is, of course, when you want to raise money from a business lender to buy a company or to expand it.

If you remember a point made in the chapter on financing, it only makes sense to deal with a business bank, and provide the loan officer a copy of your financials, if you are unable or unwilling to put up real estate or a saving account as security for the loan. Otherwise, I think it's easiest and most sensible to go for a simple home equity loan from one of the many lenders who offer competitive rates in that marketplace. In that event you can leave your business plan at home.

But if your approach is to get the funds you need solely on the strength of the business and on the quality of your forecasting and business planning, then it's your plan that will be the key to access the money.

Another intelligent way to use your plan is to share it – after removing sensitive and confidential information – with employees, even vendors and customers. Allowing these people, who are important to your business' success, to visualize your business –

its strengths, its future and its values – the way you do, is likely to impact, in a positive way, their allegiance to your firm. Having thought about and defined what you want to accomplish enables you to more readily articulate your objectives and your methods to others. And it's probable the more they understand about what you want to accomplish, the more likely they will be to assist you.

Conclusion

I am a strong advocate for the idea that owners of small California businesses should develop the ability to prepare plans for their companies. The process itself is invaluable if you want to be a success in your business, and the plan is helpful – some think it is critical – if you want to get a business loan or to share with others – employees, customers and vendors – your vision for your company, so that they are encouraged to work cooperatively with you toward the achievement of your business' goals.

KEY POINTS FROM THIS CHAPTER

❖ *It's recommended that once you find a business you like, you spend time thinking about the markets it serves, the characteristics that make it unique, and the problems that might be encountered. Then develop a plan to maximize its strengths and address its challenges.*

❖ *If you want to set your company apart from most others, take the simple step of adopting the discipline of formal, systematic and regular planning.*

❖ *Proper planning can aid in the effort to keep a company moving forward toward specific objectives without sacrificing the "dexterity" necessary for survival in the contemporary business environment.*

❖ *But just because planning is the "simple" solution, does not make it "easy" to implement, which may be why many business people acknowledge the importance of preparation but neglect to practice it consistently.*

❖ *Getting in the habit of planning helps to develop a "way of thinking" about a business that can lead to success.*

❖ *Don't be intimidated by the business planning process or worried that you don't have solutions for all the problems anticipated. Business planning is a skill that is refined over time and the solutions will come to you as you learn to tap resources that yield answers to your questions.*

❖ *The first element of a business plan is a clearly stated objective that is measurable, ambitious, achievable and includes a deadline.*

❖ *A general description of your company helps you to assess all of the assets and problems that you face as its owner.*

❖ *External circumstances that should be noted in a business plan are the factors in the environment in which the company operates – factors over which you don't have much control. They include the market for your goods and services, the competitive situation, the employee pool.*

❖ *Internal factors influencing the success of your business include issues of employees, expenses, suppliers and the matters over which you do have control. That problems in this area are not always dealt with promptly may mean you don't care to face difficult decisions. Perhaps you need to adopt a bolder style of management, exhibiting the courage to do what needs to be done.*

❖   *The most obvious practical purpose for your business plan is, of course, to present to a lender when requesting money to purchase or expand a business.*

❖   *Another intelligent way to use your plan is to share its visions, ideas and objectives with those who can help you achieve the objectives – your employees, customers and suppliers.*

Business Plan for City Coffee Services, San Jose California
December, 2004

(This is a fictional company and a fictional plan, but based on a composite of actual companies and business planning approaches.)

OBJECTIVE

Maintain revenues in Calendar 2005 at the same level as 2004 revenues, and increase earnings in Calendar 2005 by 20% compared to 2004 earnings, despite the slowdown in the industry and less demand for our products and services.

BACKGROUND

City Coffee was established in 1996 to provide gourmet office coffee products and services for businesses, primarily offices, in the Santa Clara Valley. It was started by one individual, the owner, who solicited business, set up new accounts with brewing equipment and then delivered coffee and ancillary items (sugars, creamers, napkins and so forth) in a single van. One employee was hired at the beginning to work in the office part time answering phones, handling billings, making deposits and managing related activities. He also spent part time in the warehouse putting away deliveries, packing orders, maintaining inventory, etc. The company generated a little under $100,000 that first year.

At present the company shows revenues and earnings substantially greater than when it started. It has enjoyed continued expansion in the number of customers, the size of their orders, and the extent of products and services. Much of the growth resulted from the acquisition, in 1999, of a vending company and all its equipment. Purpose was to (1) get the acquired company's (few) coffee accounts, to (2) provide coffee service to the new vending accounts and to (3) add the vending capability for established coffee-only accounts.

In addition to the working owner there are two full-time employees and one part time employee, providing customers with a variety of coffees, teas and ancillary supplies, and filling and servicing more than 100 vending machines providing soft drinks, cookies and snacks for some of the accounts. There are a total of 96 accounts in Santa Clara County.

The firm occupies a facility which includes a warehouse and offices, covering 2,700 square feet at a market rate of rent. It has been at the location for three years and has a lease and option for the next seven years.

CHALLENGES AND OPPORTUNITIES

Because of the economic slowdown in 2000 and 2001, many of the companies which purchased items from City Coffee to provide perks for employees (at the time, it was difficult to get and retain good employees) ended that practice. Also, many of the accounts have laid off employees (with the result that there are fewer coffee and vending customers) and some of the users of the vending machines may be watching their expenditures more closely and are not purchasing impulse snack items as readily as they did.

Business declined at City Coffee in 2001 and 2002, compared to 2000, and there has been no increase in revenues in 2003 or 2004. Earnings performance has pretty closely tracked sales.

Inherent in the conditions causing these problems, however, are opportunities. They are detailed as follows:

External Factors: Influences outside the company over which we have little control and yet which impact City Coffee customers and can impact the company's business.

Challenges

• Business decline because of reduction in work force among clients, some (former) clients no longer take our service. Consequently, City Coffee has less business and finds it difficult to obtain new clients.

• Economic forecasts indicate the slow business conditions will not improve appreciably in 2005.

• Increased competitive pressure from other companies in this business and this area, which are eager for business so are making promises and offering discounts in order to lure our customers away.

• Some of our vendors who sell us coffee, ancillary products, supplies and the snack and soft drink items sold through the vending machines are insistent on being paid for product upon delivery. They are concerned because some customers have gone out of business owing them money. One result of their policies is that City Coffee can no longer pay for products with the revenues collected from the sale of those products. Instead, the products have to be paid for before they can be sold

Opportunities

• In this economic environment, it's not likely we'll face any price increases from vendors or service providers. That includes the rent on the warehouse/office space and also includes wages. (But we do expect cost increases in some areas such as Worker's Compensation insurance premiums and gasoline.)

- Borrowing money may be relatively easy for healthy companies with growth plans because while business banks want to provide loans, many of their prospective customers are not good credit risks due to the problems they are having during the current economic circumstances.

- By "reshopping" for our services, such as shipping, equipment repair, etc., we may be able to find vendors willing to offer us excellent pricing, lower than our current prices, to get our business.

- Companies smaller than City Coffee are having a particularly difficult time and may be motivated to sell out.

Internal Factors: Circumstances within the company over which management has a great deal of control.

Challenges

- Equipment is getting older and will necessitate more repairs. Of particular concern is the oldest van, which may need replacement in a few months.

- Employee morale is negatively affected by the slowed business climate. It impacts productivity and some of the pessimism is expressed to clients.

- One of the route drivers is decidedly less productive than he used to be, much less productive than the others. He claims to have family problems. There are signs he is abusing drugs when not at work. He has been responsible for our getting a number of parking tickets and because he didn't notify us about them, the company was charged substantial penalties by the traffic and parking authorities.

- There has been substantial profit drainage the past few years due to sloppy practices. The parking tickets and penalties is one example.

- We have put off updating our accounting and customer management software with the result that the current system is a patchwork of computerized data and paper records. It is slow and inefficient. Mistakes are easily made.

Opportunities

- As there are few job openings in this business at present, we're not likely to lose any of our employees. Any open positions could be readily filled with a fully-competent person.

- Just as this could be a good time to buy or lease equipment for use in route operations, it also could be a good time to upgrade company infrastructure.

STRATEGIES

To address the challenges and opportunities, the following strategies are recommended. Included are the time objectives.

- Customer appreciation visits, meetings with customers by City Coffee owner to be completed by 3/31/05 will seek to let customers know they are appreciated, make sure they are satisfied with our service, find out if there are problems or complaints, learn what else we can do for them, learn (if possible) what they are being told by competitors to lure them away. Purpose of this program is to prevent the loss of more clients.

- Provide customers ways to reduce their costs as part of customer appreciation visits. Cost reduce methods include cut back in our service (fewer calls per month), recommend they discontinue their 100% subsidized coffee and snacks policies (and require employees to pay a small amount for what they consumer), change the product they receive (such as replacing gourmet coffees with standard brands), provide a discount for paying our bills within three days of invoice.

- Eliminate sloppy practices to the extent we can so as to eliminate unnecessary expenses. Owner to discuss with employees and ask for suggestions (so it is their program), at least once every quarter.

- Owner to contact suppliers of products and supplies by 1/31/05 to learn if they will provide reduction in prices to keep our business. What about if we pay more promptly?

- Owner to determine if we can save enough by more prompt payment to vendors to warrant borrowing the money needed to facilitate the faster payoff.

- Office manager to investigate and select one of the mobile phone service carriers advertising substantially lower prices than we're paying. Goal is to reduce overall phone expense by 10%.

- Owner to let employees know, in bi-monthly letters and quarterly meetings that we are doing a good job of solving problems and taking care of accounts. They should be proud of our company and reflect that in their conversations with customers.

- Owner and office manager to develop a more aggressive accounts receivables management program by 1/20/05 so that customers are not able to owe us as much money for so long, or to fail to pay. Goal is to make more "collection" calls, switch late paying accounts to C.O.D. basis sooner than we have in the past, in order to reduce bad debt by 50% compared to 2004.

- Owner to lay off weakest employee by 1/15/04, he'll be paid through 1/31/05. This is slower time of year and we can manage for 30 days with the one fewer employee, then begin interviewing in March to have replacement in place by 4/1/05. To speak with lawyer by 1/10/05 to develop proper strategy for laying off employee and minimize risk of termination lawsuit.

- Owner to shop for new van and determine whether to lease or buy after speaking with accountant. This to be completed by 2/15/05. Purchase of van to be completed by 2/28/05.

- Owner to find a source to refinance company debt by 1/31/05. Goal is to reduce interest expenses by 20%, which, according to the information received in recent solicitations from lenders, is a realistic goal. This business plan to be used in the loan application package.

- Owner to meet with client prospect in the IT business which is interested in a trade of their older programs (but may do just what we need) and their IT support to solve our accounting problems, in exchange for us placing three vending machines (that are now gathering dust in the warehouse) at their office and servicing them weekly.

Additionally (if possible):

- Acquire smaller company by 6/30/05 to add income without corresponding increase in costs, as we would use existing infrastructure (with, perhaps incremental changes) to manage additional business. To accomplish this objective, owner to engage business broker by 1/15/05 to conduct search. Also begin putting out the word among industry contacts immediately that City Coffee is looking to acquire another company. Other items to handle to reach this objective include establishing specific criteria for acquisition by 1/31/05, and talking to three or four lenders to learn how much we can borrow and to get pre-qualified by 2/15/05.

- Interview sales representatives to determine if there is one we can afford who can do a good job of building our business. This is a project for the second half of 2005.

• Investigate, in the second half of 2005, the idea of a profit sharing program for employees beginning in 2006.

NOTES

The financial material that follows includes the projected (2004) year end results for City Coffee Services and a single possible projection, reflecting the changes anticipated by adding business and reducing costs, and projecting the effects of these changes in terms of meeting our objective.

INCOME			ADDED EXPENSES EXPECTED		PLANNED 2005 SAVINGS	
Vending Product Sales	39,450	6				
Office Coffee Product	333,301.38	50.9				
CCS Vending Accounts	266,956.28	40.8				
Machine/Equip Rentals	27,265	4.2				
Catering	38.6	0				
Parts Sales	1,080.69	0.2				
Refurbushing		0				
Installs fees	4.19	0				
Monthly Rentals	4,098	0.6				
Labor Machine Fills	8,635.80	1.3				
Sales Tax Paid	-26,078.39	-4				
TOTAL INCOME	**654,751.55**	**100**				
COST OF SALES						
Cost of Goods Sold	267,771.80	40.9				
Repairs	1,389.28	0.2				
Commissions	2,295.92	0.4				
Payroll - Employees	72,304.83	11				
Payroll Tax Expense	6,884.40	1				
TOTAL COST OF SALES	**350,606.23**	**53.5**				
GROSS PROFIT	**304,145.32**	**46.5**				
OPERATING EXPENSES						
Accounting	15,859.54	2.4				
Advertising	-173	0				
Auto Expense	5,996.12	0.9	Replace Van and Higher gas prices	3,600.00		
Auto Insurance	9,325.94	1.4	Higher cost with new vehicle	800		
Banking Fees	3,473.27	0.5				
Bad Debts	32,154.58	4.9			Reduce by 50%	16,077.29
Casual Labor	10,895.00	1.7				
Donations	100.00	0				
Dues & Subscriptions	205.00	0				
Entertainment	8,025.71	1.2				
Equipment Lease	1,528.02	0.2				
Freight & Delivery	114.88	0				
House Parts	705.60	0.1				
Insurance - Gen Liability	6,276.73	1				
Insurance - Health	7,173	1.1				
Insurance - Work Comp	5,016.94	0.8	Anticipated Increase	700		
Interest	9.89	0				
Interest - Loans	24,409.82	3.7			Interest reduce by 20%	4,881.96
Interest - Credit Cards	99.58	0			Eliminate	99.58
Late Fees	1,787.78	0.3				
Legal	522.00	0.1				
Office Supplies	3,246.77	0.5				
Penalties	139.98	0			Eliminate	139.88
Postage	520.90	0.1				
Rent	19,888	3				
Repairs & Maintenance	407.31	0.1				
Security	-149.82	0				
Telephone	12,401.92	1.9			New Mobile Phone Plan	1,240.19
Travel	1,469.58	0.2				
Uniforms	110.22	0				
Utilities	2,509.24	0.4				
TOTAL OPERATING EXPENSES	**174,050.50**	**26.6**				
NET INCOME FROM OPERATIONS	**130,094.82**	**19.9**	**INCREASED COSTS**	**5,100.00**	**TOTAL SAVINGS**	**22,438.90**
Payroll Clearing	-37.41	0				
Officer's Life Insurance	1,120.00	0.2				
Amortization Expense	-4,424.20	-0.7				
Deptreciation Expense	-52,782.00	-8.1				
Trade-in Auto	18,631.31	2.8				
Suspense	0.00	0				
TOTAL OTHER INCOME & EXPENSES	**-37,492.30**	**-5.7**				
EARNINGS BEFORE TAX	**92,602.52**	**14.1**			**NET IMPROVEMENT**	**17,338.90**
NET INCOME	**92,602.52**	**14.1**				

CHAPTER ELEVEN

GETTING THE MONEY

Perhaps the first challenge you'll encounter if you've discovered an interesting business to purchase, is meeting the price, or coming close enough that the seller is willing to work with you. As noted, one of the ways you can prepare for this is to talk to your bank and get a letter stating you will be able to obtain a loan for some of the purchase price you'll need. That will help you to impress a seller when negotiating for your purchase. But remember that officers of the financial institution will want to examine the subject business and determine how much you might qualify to borrow for that purpose. So, while this approach is helpful, there is no guarantee that it will solve the problem.

Seller Financing

The number one source of funding to facilitate the sale of a small California business is, as you may have guessed, seller financing. In roughly 60% of the instances of small business sales in California, some of the money needed to complete the purchase has come from the seller. The standard arrangement is for the buyer to give the seller a cash down payment for whatever amount the parties have agreed on in their negotiations. Typically, a down payment is between one-third and one-half of the purchase price. Then, if the seller is willing to carry the balance, the buyer will issue a promissory note for that amount in favor of the seller. In most cases, the obligation will call for equal monthly payments over an agreed-on period – often three to seven years – to be paid with interest at the going market rate charged on the unpaid balance. Security for this obligation might be the assets of the business only, or a combination of the business and other property owned by the buyer.

I'm a strong advocate of seller financing as I believe it's an important ingredient in the success of a business that has changed hands. And clearly the offering of seller financing when the company is being marketed gives you and other prospective buyers the idea that it must be a solid business with a good future. After all, the seller is willing to lend money on it and he – or she – should know!

In fact, the seller not only is casting a vote of confidence for the business by offering to help finance the deal, but also is demonstrating an intent to stay involved in the fortunes of the business. If you have an obligation to the seller, that person will be inclined to offer ideas or advice to make sure the company continues to thrive, and can generate the revenues needed for you to pay it off.

Seller financing, of course, can take several forms and need not constitute the entire balance of the purchase price, after the down payment. I've been involved in transactions that used seller financing with some adjustments on the usual theme in order to accommodate the circumstances of the purchase. In one variation, the seller may wait three or six months before the payments begin. This gives the buyer an opportunity to get both feet on the ground in the company, take care of any unexpected cash requirements (there always seem to be a few of those), and to put a few dollars into building up the business. Another alternative is for the seller to receive proceeds due on the note in one or more balloon payments, rather than in monthly installments. This plan works well in a situation where a buyer intends to obtain other financing on the business, or to use different means to raise the funds within a year or so of the transfer. In effect, this tactic is calling on the seller to provide a swing loan – some money to tide the buyer over and complete the purchase – until arrangements can be made for more permanent financing. The seller in this example is not actually giving funds to the buyer, but is postponing collection of money owed, earning some interest on it and giving the buyer time to get the funds needed to retire or pay down the debt to the seller.

I've also seen seller financing structured with more than one note issued by a buyer in favor of the seller. This strategy combines standard seller financing—using a note paid in monthly installments over an agree-on period – with a note due to be retired in six or 12 months. And in one case I know about – in which the seller took a note from a buyer who planned to build up the business for resale, the parties agreed the note would be paid off with accrued interest upon the next sale of the business, whenever that might be.

Along with help financing purchase of the business, the seller often provides other benefits to the buyer, including the offer of advice, if needed, as well as some flexibility in working out the terms of the deal.

While some consultants advise sellers to get every scrap of collateral available when carrying back financing for the buyer, others feel that asking for security beyond the business itself is likely to discourage a buyer from wanting to deal.

My thought is that the way to collateralize such a loan is dependent on a number of factors. If there is a substantial down payment in relation to the size of the obligation to the seller, it probably is unnecessary to collateralize the note on the remaining sum – besides assets of the business. That's certainly the case if there is enough value in the business assets – equipment, receivables and inventory – to support the amount due.

A highly leveraged deal, however, is likely to cause a seller to worry about the possibility that the buyer can't make the business successful enough to support the debt load. If your deal is shaping up in a way that leaves the seller vulnerable to loss in the event the business goes under, you may be asked to put up real estate as added collateral in order to achieve a transaction. As noted earlier, you should determine if you are willing to do this, and how much of your personal property will be pledged for this purpose.

And you should keep in mind that there can be flexibility in this area. Parts of the collateral can be released over the period of an obligation as it becomes "seasoned." In one case, a five year note was initially secured by the business as well as the buyer's real property. After 18 months of prompt payments on the obligation, it was rewritten to require only the business assets as collateral. I believe this arrangement was needlessly complicated, but it made a deal possible for parties who were split on the issue of using the real estate security for the note. This was the compromise both could accept.

Because your best source of financing is the seller of the business, I advocate that you work with the seller to find an arrangement that makes you both feel comfortable and allows you to borrow some of your purchase price from the person who knows the business best.

The Cheapest Conventional Money

While seller financing is likely the best deal a buyer can get on funds needed to complete a purchase, the least costly loan from a conventional source is usually the home equity line offered by many banks and savings and loan institutions.

I particularly like the idea of borrowing on home equity, not only because the rates beat business loans, but also because the real estate lending route involves less red tape, requires less reporting and usually gets approved and funded more quickly than most other kinds of business loans. If a buyer has real estate with a value exceeding its mortgages, and a fairly good credit record, there are dozens of financial institutions ready to provide the cash for whatever purpose the borrower wishes to put it.

Many buyers reject this idea because they think simply that they ought to get a business loan to accomplish business purposes. In the case of most loans to purchase a business, however, the borrower is required to put up real property equity as collateral. That's right: When a business bank is called on to lend capital that will go into the down payment on a small company, the borrower is probably going to be asked to put up a second trust deed in the family home, so the lender is protected in the event the business is unable to provide the money needed to service the loan.

It doesn't take a shrewd business mind to figure out that if your real estate equity needs to be pledged anyway, you might as well get regular home equity money with the lower rates and all the other borrower benefits that come with it.

Bizbuyfinancing.com

For many business buyers, the most logical source of funding to complete a purchase is accessed on the Internet at *www.bizbuyfinancing.com* Offering connection to lenders who specialize in business purchase loans, along with timely advice, help with pre-qualification, a loan payment calculator and other useful tools, this web site should be visited by those who anticipate the need for financial assistance to buy a small California business and want useful information as well as competitive rates from experienced business lenders.

Traditional Sources

Among the most common institutional sources of money for a business acquisition is represented by the network of lenders backed by the SBA (U.S. Small Business Administration). The federal agency will guarantee loans made to purchasers and existing owners of enterprises that comply with its small business definition (up to 500 employees for most companies in manufacturing, a maximum of 100 employees in wholesale trades, a lid on annual revenues – averaged over a three-year period – of $6 million for most firms in retail and service industries, $28.5 million for the majority of businesses involved in general and heavy construction, and $12 million for special trade contractors). A benefit of this program is that borrowers without real estate for collateral still can meet the government agency's qualifications. And with this approval, many institutions will ratify loan requests up to $250,000. But if there are real estate or other available assets in the borrower's portfolio, besides the business, the lenders usually insist on using such assets – up to the value of the loan – as additional security.

What the SBA looks at are four key factors, and at least three of the four should be present for you to qualify with a lender who'll seek the SBA guarantee, and therefore will be more likely to work with you than a conventional bank. The factors are: 1. Cash flow of the business; 2. Borrower's work experience as it relates to the business; 3. Borrower's credit history; and 4. Collateral of the borrower, in addition to the business assets, that can be used to secure the obligation.

If you have what it takes to satisfy the SBA, you may be able to tap this resource for the money needed to complete a purchase. Check out the Resources Section at *www.bizben.com* for an SBA lender contact from whom you can learn more.

Buyers preparing their application for SBA backed money can ask the seller to supply information about the business. Then you would add a description of your work history and a business plan.

Money also is available from some business lenders who will take the company's liquid assets as collateral. It's common for owners of established retail firms to use inventory financing. The money helps them stock up for the holiday selling season, for example. And the inventory either is pledged to the lender to make sure the loan will be retired, or is signed over to the lender, and then released in increments back to the borrower, in return for progress payments.

Receivables financing is another way of using liquid assets to raise capital. Owners of many distribution and manufacturing businesses find that although the company is enjoying good revenues with satisfactory profit margins, most of the earnings are tied up in receivables. Until customers pay their bills, the business might be strapped for the cash needed to expand production, modernize facilities or market more aggressively. One way to improve cash flow in this situation is to pledge the receivables to a business lender for a loan of up to 80% of the value of those receivables. As the company collects the funds owed to it, the loan balance is paid down. And some firms are able to pass along to their slow-paying customers, their cost of borrowing in the form of a one or two percentage point financing charge.

A variation on this idea is for the company to sell its receivables to a factor – someone who'll pay, somewhere between 60% and 80% of the face receivables value, and then will be responsible for getting customers to pay up.

These are fairly common practices used by established businesses with existing lender relationships to ease occasional cash crunches. But there's no reason you can't ask a business bank to put up some of the money that will be used for the purchase of the company, and to accept the company's liquid assets for collateral. Inventory or receivables loans may not generate as much cash as a typical SBA-backed lending deal. But for part of a purchase price or for working capital, this may be an ideal source.

An appropriate choice of a bank might be the one now serving the business you want to buy. Ask your seller to tell his or her contact at the company's bank that you will be its new customer if it can help make the deal with a loan secured by the business' liquid assets.

Innovative Financing Strategies

As owner of a small business, you'll be confronted with challenges which are best met using resourceful planning and creative problem solving. You may get the chance to begin developing those skills if you're trying to complete a purchase, need a little more cash to accomplish that goal, and find the money is not available from

nal sources.

Just because your bank isn't willing to come up with the $10,000 or $30,000 or whatever you'll need to make the deal, doesn't mean you can't get a "yes" to this proposal by going elsewhere. Other banks, eager for new business, are one alternate source. Another is the vendors who supply your future business with the products, materials and services that enable it to function. If they would like to keep doing business with the company, once you take over, perhaps they'll be willing to stretch out the period during which they usually require their bills to be paid.

Ask the grocery wholesaler providing much of the inventory for the corner market you are buying if they can wait 45, instead of 15 days to get paid for package and dairy goods. That concession will give you a little extra money for start up expenses and working capital needs. You can then use some of your cash to meet the seller's down payment requirement.

A variation on this plan is for one or more of the business' vendors to let you pay the seller's old bills. If the seller of the photo lab you are buying, for example, owes $25,000 to an outfit which handles the high resolution scanning and digitizing work, perhaps you can take on this responsibility. And find out if the terms of payment can be extended. If so, that $25,000 will not be needed immediately for operations, so it can be used to make the deal and close the escrow. Or it is $25,000 less you have to produce for the down payment if it would have been earmarked, by the seller, for handling the payable. In other words, the seller is giving the payable to you, and he or she will need $25,000 less at close of escrow.

It should be noted that new businesses typically have been granted little in the way of credit by suppliers until there has been a track record established of prompt and consistent payment. But in the post dot-com economy, most companies are re-examining old practices in order to remain competitive. If you have good credit, you may be able to persuade vendors of your new business that they'll have to work with you in order to retain your business.

A completely different approach to accessing additional funds is to roll over your IRA or 401K funds into a trust, under the tax law that now permits funds in a trust to be used for purchase of a business without liability for deferred taxes. A provision of the U.S. Tax Code recognizes the rollover of invested funds into a business opportunity as a transaction that does not interfere with the deferred status of the taxpayer's money. This is a move that may make it possible for you to "find" several thousand more dollars to put into the purchase.

If none of these strategies will get you the down payment you need, how about putting the amount of the shortfall into a promissory note, which the seller can then discount and sell in a few months to get his or his or her cash? For sake of discussion, let's assume you can put up $150,000 of the $200,000 down payment required by the seller. Where will the other $50,000 come from? The strategy suggested here is that you pay that amount in the form of the note and then, after the note has had a chance to "season" – with all payments made promptly for six or nine months – the seller can ask a note "buy-back" company to take over as the creditor. The buy-back service then gives the seller the going rate – probably 80% ($40,000) for the "paper." This enables your seller to receive most of the down payment requested. He or she will just have to wait awhile to collect the part that wasn't available when the deal was closed.

You can explain to your seller that a benefit of this plan is there is no uncertainty about cashing in after a few months. The seller can work things out at close of escrow by contacting organizations which buy back promissory notes of this type. They will be able to find out what size note can be sold and at what discount rate. The seller can even furnish the buy-back organization with the information needed about the business for a "pre-approval" on the note purchase. Some of the most active note buy-back services can be found by checking out the resources section at *www.bizben.com*

If all else fails, there's one other source of capital which – though I consider it to be the "bank of last resort" – is commonly used by small business buyers and owners to raise money, fast. It involves a plea to the friendly lenders who fill our mail boxes with Visa and Master Card offers. Keep this in mind when you think there is no other place to get that last $10,000 or $20,000 needed to close the deal. Most likely there is.

Credit card borrowing comes at a high interest rate to be sure, but if the sum standing between you and the business you want can be accessed easily with the plastic in your wallet – and if you are sufficiently motivated to take over the business – it's a strategy worth considering.

A Note of Caution

After reviewing these suggestions about ways that you can incur additional debt to come up with all the cash needed to buy the business, you might want to take a pencil and paper to the problem so you can determine if you realistically can incur all of these obligations with the cash flow from the business.

Just how much debt do you think the business will be able to reasonably support? For the first several months after you start, you probably won't make as much money as did the seller, particularly considering the deposits and start-up expenses that will pop up in the early months of the new ownership. And then there is the cost of the mistakes that you are bound to make while learning the business.

If your seller has a firm grasp of reality, he or she will not encourage you to try and pull off a highly leveraged deal on the company. The seller stands to lose as much as you do if you aren't able to keep the company going.

Whether the company you buy is highly successful or barely getting by, the odds are against you succeeding at buying and building it up with insufficient cash. In many cases the over leveraged deal results in the company collapsing under the weight of its own debt. If your new business is over encumbered and under performing, what you have at risk is your down payment, your personal assets and the time you will invest in this project.

While I advocate that buyers look into all avenues for raising money so as to complete the purchase, these ideas should be tempered with the your good judgment about the possibilities of loss and the risks you're willing to take.

Shared Equity

One final strategy can work out well if you're not prepared to buy the business all at once, but have the trust of the seller. You can form a partnership or a corporation in which you take over some or most of the ownership, conduct most of the work and take most of the responsibility. The seller can stay on as your partner, take an appropriate salary and you can complete the buyout over time, as you generate the money with your work, and from your share of the profits.

There are any number of ways to structure such a deal, and plenty of attorneys, bankers, insurance agents (who will arrange to underwrite a buy/sell agreement triggered by the death or illness of you or the seller), and other consultants who can help you make this happen. That's really the easy part.

The critical question is whether there is enough trust and communication between you and your seller to make this work.

This strategy is not, of course, as easy and quick as an outright purchase. But if there is a solid connection with the seller and you really want the business, the two of you should explore the idea of "sharing" the company for awhile.

Conclusion

While getting ready to buy your small California business you're wise to give some thought as to how you will pay for it. Where will you source additional capital, if needed, to close a deal?

My favorite, of course, is seller financing. That's the easiest, quickest way to go. And I believe the best deals – the ones that prove successful for the buyer and the seller – are those in which the person from whom you bought the business has a stake in the future of your success.

Among other suggestions offered are the traditional resources for business capital including SBA secured money, cash advanced on liquid assets of the business and – perhaps surprisingly – a simple home equity loan. Among the less common techniques are tapping vendors for extensions on the time needed for the business to pay off its accounts payables, and rolling over one or more of your retirement accounts into tax-protected trusts that can help fund a business purchase.

KEY POINTS FROM THIS CHAPTER

❖ *The number one source of funding to facilitate the sale of a small California business – accounting for about 60% of the deals – is seller financing of at least some of the money needed.*

❖ *Seller financing offers a number of advantages in the way it adds to the appeal of the business. And it frequently provides affordable purchase money for the buyer.*

❖ *The question of whether to collateralize the note to the seller with business assets only, or with other property you have, is often a point for negotiation when seller financing is involved. There is no single right solution for this matter and you are advised to try and work out a mutually acceptable plan that balances risk and reward for you and the seller.*

❖ *The cheapest conventional way to borrow is usually with a home equity loan – a preferable deal to most loan packages granted to buy a business. The later come with higher interest rates and more qualifying and reporting requirements, along with the need to put up the same real estate collateral used to secure simple home equity financing.*

❖ *For many business buyers the best resource to find additional money for completing a purchase, in addition to useful information and other valuable online finance tools, can be found at www.bizbuyfinancing.com*

❖ *One approach to getting an institutional loan for a business purchase, without real estate security, is the program offered by the Federal Government through the SBA. It guarantees business loans from select institutions to those who qualify. Buyers can learn more about getting access to SBA-backed funds by going to the Resources Section at www.bizben.com*

❖ *Lenders who provide receivables or inventory financing might be resources for some of the cash needed to complete the sale of a small California business.*

❖ *Another way to fund part of the seller's down payment is to pre-qualify with one of the services which buy back promissory notes. The seller can discount and sell a note received from you after six or nine months of "seasoning." The seller can "pre qualify" the business for this strategy, so as to be ready when it's time to sell the note. Some of these services also are found in the Resources Section at www.bizben.com*

❖ *Vendors to the business can be a source of financing if they will agree to let you take responsibility for the seller's payables. This strategy frees up cash to increase the down payment or working capital. Vendors also can cooperate with you, the new buyer, by permitting an extension in payment of their obligations.*

❖ *You also may be able to get funding by rolling over your retirement account into a trust that can be used to buy a business without triggering any tax consequences.*

❖ *The "bank of last resort," using credit cards, is sometimes the solution for a buyer who needs more cash to complete a deal and has no other resources.*

❖ *Buyers are cautioned about getting too creative in finding money for a leveraged purchase. Don't put yourself and the seller at risk of your becoming overburdened with debt that must be serviced by income from a business which you still are learning to operate.*

❖ *If a buyer can't raise enough money through increased debt to buy all of a business, one solution is to buy part or most of the business and become partners or a corporate shareholder with the seller.*

CHAPTER TWELVE

THE OFFER

If your search is going particularly well, you may have encountered an interesting company you'd like to own after just a few weeks of looking at small California businesses for sale. More likely it's been several months of reviewing opportunities that have seemed unappealing or over-priced. Or both. But at last you seem to have discovered a company which meets your needs and has potential for growth.

Whether you're in for a long search or a short one, if and when you're introduced to an opportunity that appears to line up favorably with your criteria, it's important that you make out a check to an escrow company that handles business transactions, and then prepare an offer to buy the business.

Incidentally, your business broker or agent (if you're working with one) can recommend an escrow holder. Or you can find these services listed in the resources section at *www.bizben.com*

Letter of Intent

An alternative to the offer is a Letter of Intent (LOI), which is commonly used for larger (one-half million dollars and up) and more complicated transactions. The LOI is rarely binding on the buyer unless it specifically states that acceptance on the part of the seller will obligate them both to perform. The purpose of the LOI is to establish the basic components of what will be the transaction, and determine if buyer and seller are in agreement on the terms of a deal, before they move forward with preparation of a purchase contract. It's the first draft of an agreement, stating the intention of the parties to have a deal as outlined.

This might be an appropriate document to use as your first written expression of interest in a company that you expect to acquire in a corporate stock purchase. And the LOI procedure, followed by an attorney-written contract, is the solution if there will be complex issues or several conditions – examples are an extended escrow, the required approval of other buyers, a drawn-out due diligence period – that are too involved to be adequately covered with the standard purchase form.

In other words, if your attorney will be asked to prepare the actual agreement, it will be based on principles and language derived from your LOI to the seller.

The Offer Includes

A standard offer form is used for most transactions involving small California businesses. And once approved, it becomes the purchase agreement, as it spells out all the terms by which the parties agree to transact business. And whether using a Letter of Intent or a standard offer, you will include the same basic provisions. They are:

- Identity of parties (buyer and seller)

- Name and address of the subject business

- Sales price

- Cash down payment

- Buyer's assumption of obligations

- Terms of payment of balance due to seller

- Assets included

- Assets not included

- Seller agreements: including covenant not to compete and training

- Buyer agreements: including non-disclosure

- Method of handling such matters as inventory, payables, receivables, deposits

- Contingencies: including approvals of third parties, such as landlord, franchisor, lenders and creditors of the seller

- Buyer due diligence

- Seller due diligence

- Time considerations/deadlines

- Name of escrow holder

- Determination of who will pay for escrow (usually: 50/50)

- List of items to be completed in escrow and documents to be prepared by escrow holder

- Payment of fees to broker(s)

- Representations and warranties

- Legal language including provisions about treatment of deposit, consequences of breach, procedure in the event of disputes (court or arbitration?).

There are a number of existing forms which you can use to establish a legal purchase agreement that work fine in most transactions involving small California businesses. One example can be found at the *www.bizben.com* site. Select "Forms" and download the Conditional Purchase and Sale of Assets Agreement.

To make your offer more persuasive, it's a good idea to present it with a copy of your resume, your financial statement and credit report. And if you've arranged to borrow extra funds, if needed, you can include a letter from an officer of the bank, stating that you are pre-approved for a loan of a certain sum to aid in the purchase of a business, subject to the bank's satisfactory review of the deal.

The seller should be granted a specific amount of time, usually two to four days, to respond, either by signing the offer as is, which makes it a contract, or by preparing a counter offer. In that event the seller usually will sign under the phrase "subject to counteroffer dated (date is specified)." That places the ball back in your court. You will have a few days to accept the agreement, as changed by the seller's counter offer, or to agree – but subject to your own counter offer.

The exchange of counteroffers, if that continues, can get a little unwieldy and confusing. You or the seller may forget where you stand with respect to various issues if you keep sending the agreement back and forth with more revisions.

The recommended procedure, after the third or fourth counteroffer has been presented by an intermediary, if it appears you both want to try and come to a mutual agreement, is to meet and negotiate each of the items that need to be resolved. And it's best to have a skilled negotiator, perhaps your broker or the one representing the seller, to assist in the work of reaching an understanding acceptable to both.

You'll get a chance to learn a bit about negotiations in the following chapter.

What You Want

You probably know that two honest, well meaning people can look at the same situation and come away with different ideas about it. That's why it's a good idea for you to be thorough and explicit in describing what you expect to be included in the business that you propose to buy. You probably will want:

Business name and trade style

It's surprising how many purchase contracts neglect to mention that the name of the business and its trade style, or logo, are included in the deal and should belong to the buyer when he or she takes over. That goes for the phone number as well. It may be understood that these are part of the goodwill, but it doesn't hurt to make the intention clear. I'm familiar with transactions that stumbled over what should be this obvious factor. In one case the seller announced that he was planning to open a day care facility for dogs in another California city under the same trade name. His new enterprise would be far enough away from the business he was selling that there would be no violation of his covenant not to compete. But he claimed that if the buyer operated under his name and earned a bad reputation with poor service, it would reflect negatively on the seller's new business. He told the buyer that she could have all the other assets of the business, but not the business' name. This disclosure came at the very last minute, but the buyer declined to proceed with the transaction under those circumstances. Much time and unrefundable escrow and due diligence expenses were spent unnecessarily. The disagreement would have been confronted at the beginning of the negotiations had the buyer's intent to use the trade name been specifically stated in the offer.

Hard assets

In the category of hard assets you'll find all of the equipment used in the business, as well as the furniture, fixtures and even supplies. For a manufacturing company, or a processing business – such as a machine shop, and for certain kinds of service providers – including everything from a shoe repair shop to a hi-tech medical imaging clinic – the equipment is vital to the conduct of the business. This is even true in some service businesses where the only valuable asset is software used to manage customer accounts. The best way to be specific about what you expect to have included among the hard assets is to attach a list of everything as an exhibit or an addendum to the agreement. The list may be the one provided to you by the seller as part of the offering package. If that list is not complete, the offer should spell out the requirement that it be completed, and its contents agreed on, within a specified number of days following acceptance of the offer.

This also is the approach to take if no list exists, and you haven't had the opportunity to compile it – perhaps because you haven't been at the premises long enough to scrutinize everything in detail.

I'm reminded of a deal on a Toyota repair garage that almost wound up in court over a fight regarding the computer disks containing repair manuals. The seller maintained they were his personal property, and he needed them for reference when repairing his own car. The buyer felt that they were part of the equipment of the shop, needed for proper conduct of the business, and that the seller had no right to keep them. Besides that, they were very expensive to replace. The matter was finally resolved in favor of the buyer, but not before each party spent several hundred dollars in attorney fees.

And while it isn't necessary to count paper clips and spare rolls of toilet paper, I have seen lists that included items such as telephone, clock, waste basket and stapler. And it's useful to at least make clear the intention to include supplies by adding to your list a phrase such as: "All office and cleaning supplies ordinarily kept on premises."

Leasehold improvements also belong on the list. The legal owner of items such as refrigeration, ovens and fire security system (in the case of a restaurant), counters, shelves and lighting (in a retail store), and trade fixtures used in other businesses, should be spelled out in the lease. You want to determine if equipment and fixtures attached to the walls and ceiling, and affixed to the floor, belong to the real estate – meaning they are owned by the landlord – or to the lessee who operates the business. In either event, your agreement should specify exactly which items are to be included in the sale.

Inventory

Whether the inventory of merchandise held for resale is included in the price of the business, or is to be purchased separately by the buyer at close of escrow, should be made clear in the purchase contract. If not, a misunderstanding is almost certainly going to occur. The buyer will voice the expectation that the linens, pillows and quilts sold in the bedding store are part of what she is buying, while the seller invariably believes that the sales price is for other assets of the business, and that the wholesale value of the inventory should be calculated in addition to the business' sales price.

Does it matter to the buyer or seller whether inventory is included in the price or is added later? Ordinarily there are no substantial advantages or disadvantages using either approach. In fact, this choice is of more interest to the broker, if one is involved, because commission usually is calculated on price; the higher the sales price for the business, the large the commission. So brokers ordinarily advocate that inventory be included.

What is important to the principles, in addition to their agreement about treatment of inventory, is its value at close of escrow. This is particularly the case if inventory will be included in the price. And there should be a provision for adjusting the price upward by the amount that inventory value in the final count exceeds the value stated in the agreement. If, for example, the agreement states that the $150,000 sale price includes $22,500 of inventory at cost, and a final count reveals a total of $24,000, the sales price would be adjusted to $151,500. Of course it works the other way: The sales price would be reduced in the event inventory value at close is lower than the amount anticipated in the contract.

Regardless of whether the business' sale price includes inventory, the physical count should be conducted right before close of escrow, with both buyer and seller involved.

Once all the items have been counted and a total value calculated after consulting the price lists, the final figure is furnished to the escrow holder.

Closing instructions from escrow will have the buyer bring the specified amount in a cashier's check. Or, if parties prefer, any adjustments can be made in the face amount of the promissory note due to the seller.

Agreements with other parties

The premises lease, the Yellow Pages advertising contract and any other agreements to which the business is party should be noted in the purchase agreement and transferred to the buyer at the close of escrow. If there are exceptions to this, because there are agreements to which the new owner does not want to be obligated, those exceptions should be stated.

Does the business have marketing arrangements with other organizations? There may be sponsorship of a local sports team, a contract with a coupon distributor, a billboard deal or advertising in local periodicals and buying guides. The buyer wants to learn about all of these programs, and determine which agreements the business wants to maintain. And if possible, get confirmation from the third parties that they will continue to do business under the same terms with the new ownership.

Customer contracts ordinarily are included in the sale and should be specifically mentioned and explained in the purchase/sale agreement.

Other assets

In addition to the agreements noted above, there may be licenses, patents, franchise rights and other assets which have value and are important to the successful operation of the business. They should be specifically identified in the offer as well as in any subsequent contracts involved in the purchase of the business. The buyer will do well to verify the assignability of any agreements or rights belonging to the business being purchased. If any of the contracts with third parties are not assignable, the buyer should be aware of that so other arrangements can be made. And if certain contracts are important to the business and cannot be obtained by the buyer, it might be wise to cancel the transaction.

It's usually a good idea to attach as exhibits to the purchase contract, copies of any documentation of agreements with other parties, as well as permits, licenses, patents, exclusive marketing rights and whatever other pacts belong to, or confer rights on the business. Are they to be transferred to the new owner? By having all of these items identified in the agreement between buyer and seller, there is less chance for confusion or misunderstanding about what is included in the business sale.

Featuring the Successful bizben Method!

Seller agreements

The seller's covenant not to compete can be important to the buyer not only because of the protection it affords but also because it is an asset that can be written off in the buyer's tax returns over the life of the agreement. In the case of a three-year covenant, for example, the buyer will be able to deduct an amount equal to one third of its value from taxable profits, each year for three years.

And the training agreement, while it usually is not treated as a depreciable asset for tax purposes, can be important as an opportunity for the buyer to get a quick education about the business and to use the seller as a marketing tool. The smart buyer asks the seller to make an introduction to key customers and to provide insight into how to work with them to maximum advantage. These are assets which the buyer should make sure are clearly defined in the agreement. They can be detailed within the text of the basic contract, or can be expressed in separate documents attached as addenda to the contract.

Buyer's agreement

The buyer might want to reiterate his or her pledge to maintain the non-disclosure of the seller and the business information throughout the process of the sale.

Goodwill

Having no significant tax planning value, and representing a less tangible part of the deal than many of the other assets, the goodwill is, nevertheless, an important part of the business you are buying. Among the components considered to be included in goodwill are the company's name and reputation, and the expectation of continuing business from its customer base. This is understood more clearly by contrast with a brand new company which has not yet established an identity in the marketplace, and is still focusing its efforts on gaining customers. For a newly formed enterprise the acquisition of goodwill will require months or years of continuous effort. While it's generally understood that the company's goodwill is included in the sale, I think it's a good idea for the buyer to make sure it is referenced in the contract, as one of the business' assets being purchased.

Also to be mentioned as an asset being purchased is the customer list. This is generally considered to fall within the category of goodwill, although court cases have established the customer list – at least in some industries – to be a separate item. Make sure that you get a list of customers or a file drawer of customer account information when you take over the business. And be certain to include customer list in the purchase agreement as one of the assets that will be transferred to you.

Allocation of purchase price

It would be easy to simply assume that the sum of the values of all the assets sold is equal to the total purchase price, without assigning – or allocating – a specific value to each item.

The tax law, however, makes it mandatory that the agreement include the specific amount of the total purchase price that is allocated to each asset. And the allocation should be agreed on by both parties, even though every asset may have a different value for the buyer than for the seller.

The buyer, for example, considers the training agreement and covenant not to compete to be more valuable than does the seller. And because each has a different depreciation program, one party will consider the depreciable hard assets to be worth more than will the other party.

At issue, of course is the tax treatment for dollars allocated to these assets. What is ordinarily in the best interest of the buyer, from a tax standpoint, is contrary to what is most beneficial for the seller's tax planning strategy.

An allocation is probably included in the seller's offering package. You, the buyer, would be smart to review this information with a tax specialist before deciding whether to accept the allocation as structured by the seller, or to propose a different allocation, more favorable to your tax planning. This matter can become a subject of negotiations between buyer and seller, and should be resolved at the time the other particulars – price and terms of the transaction – are worked out. In any event, the allocation belongs in the purchase contract, either as an addendum, or it can be included in the body of the offer, and the contract.

As an example, a possible allocation for a café selling at $200,000, could be $50,000 for equipment, $25,000 for leasehold improvements, $20,000 for training, $30,000 for a three-year non-compete agreement, and the balance of $75,000 for goodwill. If this is acceptable to the parties, it would be part of their purchase agreement.

Representations and warranties

Your agreement with the seller should contain the seller's assertions that everything told to you about the business is true and accurate and that there are no material facts being withheld from you. This provision in a contract frequently is ignored or overlooked because it seems like so much "legalese."

But it's good to include this provision in your agreement because it is meant to protect you. In many cases of fraud and deception by a seller, it was a paragraph about representations and warranties which was cited by a buyer in pursuit of his or her rights.

What You Don't Want

By definition, the asset purchase that you hope to be engaged in when you've found the right business will call for you to buy the items reviewed earlier in this chapter. And you'll want to receive those assets free and clear of any liabilities, liens or encumbrances. This should be clearly specified in your agreement with the seller.

Additionally, the bulk sale procedure you'll follow when in escrow, will comply with requirements specified in the California Uniform Commercial Code to make sure there is free title to all the assets you'll receive from the seller. Any encumbrances or obligations claimed against anything you are going to purchase need to be satisfied or removed by the seller before you take over the business and its assets.

This applies also to any legal claims that might arise after you take over the business but are based in circumstances that existed before the company was yours. An illustration is the experience of a new owner in a dry cleaning business who was confronted by an unhappy customer, complaining about a sweater, worth $150, ruined by the company the week before the buyer and seller closed escrow.

The buyer insisted the problem was not his fault because the business did not belong to him when the damage occurred. The customer, predictably, stated that he didn't care who owned the business when the garment was damaged, as far as he was concerned, it was the company's fault, and he wanted the company to replace the sweater or give him $150.

The buyer wisely delegated the problem to the seller, letting him know it was his responsibility, because their agreement said the buyer would get the business free and clear of any obligations, and the seller would protect the buyer in any action of this kind.

And you want to make sure the seller has paid or agrees to take care of all of the payables that are due from the business. Some of the creditors – people or companies owed money by the business – may be regular suppliers. So it's important their bills are paid and that they intend to continue the relationship with your new business. It's not fair to you, if a vendor cuts off supplies to you because the old owner was behind in making payments.

If you do agree to assume any of the seller's obligations, you should receive a compensating benefit from the seller. In other words, if a seller owes a vendor $10,000, the buyer may want to assume that obligation in return for a $10,000 reduction in the purchase price.

It's probably best, incidentally, for the seller to keep the receivables since he or she is responsible for the payables. The money owed to the business before you take over rightfully belongs to the seller. There's no reason, however, why you can't arrange to collect from customers on their old accounts – and turn those receipts over to the seller – as you interact with these customers with new business. Just make sure they understand the payments on old business go to the seller, and they have a responsibility to remain current with you on new business.

Another way for the new owner to manage old receivables is to actually buy them at a discount from the seller, then keep the proceeds as they are collected. As an example, if the seller is carrying $5,000 in receivables, the buyer could pay $4,000 (a customary 80%) to the seller for the right to those funds. Then as the receivables are collected, they belong to the buyer.

Conclusion

Whether contained in a Letter of Intent (LOI) or a standard offer form, the statement of your terms for purchasing a small California business should be presented to the seller along with details of your work experience and financial ability. The offer includes identity of the parties and the business, description of the deal structure, reference to exhibits or addenda that detail the assets included, seller's and buyer's agreements, contingencies and a recognition of what actions need to be addressed, including the opening of escrow, in order to complete the transaction. Time requirements also are included for those responsibilities still to be completed.

The various assets that should be transferred to the buyer include tangible and intangible items and should be specified in the purchase contract. Not included should be the seller's various long-term and short-term liabilities and any encumbrances against the business.

KEY POINTS FROM THIS CHAPTER

❖ *Most offers to purchase a small California business are made on one of the standard offer forms which then constitute the contract between buyer and seller, once parties are in agreement on the terms of the deal. A sample offer form is available at www.bizben.com Select the "Forms" option and then choose and download the Conditional Purchase and Sale of Assets Agreement.*

❖ *The Letter of Intent (LOI) is used for larger and more complex transaction which will be conducted according to a purchase agreement prepared by an attorney. The LOI states the buyer's intent and helps determine if parties are in agreement before they proceed to have the contract prepared.*

❖ *The buyer is advised to submit a history of work experience and details of his or her financial ability along with the offer or LOI. This can help to per-suade the seller about the seriousness and capabilities of the buyer.*

❖ *Once presented with an offer or LOI, the seller can accept all of the terms, or reject it because of differences over some of the terms, or accept the offer subject to a counter offer, which means the seller wants to specify some alternative terms.*

❖ *The buyer also can respond with a counter offer to a counter offer from the seller. If parties want to have a transaction and yet are unable to agree on all aspects, as demonstrated by the exchange of counteroffers, the best idea might be for them to meet across the bargaining table and attempt to go over every item, one my one, until they have a complete agreement, or until they discover they are unable to come to agreement, which means they should not waste more time.*

❖ *The offer should include the identity of the parties and the business, the particulars of the proposed deal structure, and a description of what tasks and obligations need to be accomplished, and when, before the business can change hands.*

❖ *Because two reasonable and honest people still can have different interpre-tations about the meaning of an unclear provision, it is important that the offer and the purchase agreement describe, as explicitly as possible, what you expect to receive in your purchase of the business.*

❖ *Among the assets that should be specifically mentioned by the buyer as included with the sale is the business name and its trade style, or logo.*

❖ *A list of all capital assets to be sold should be included in the offer, and then in the contract. It's best if the list is as complete as parties can make it. Leasehold improvements, though a different class of assets than tools and equipment, also should be included.*

❖ *Whether or not the value of the inventory is to be included in the purchase price must be stated in the offer. Include an approximate value and note that it is subject to change, once the actual count of inventory is conducted immediately prior to close of escrow.*

❖ *The premises lease, advertising contracts, deals with customers and any other legal agreements relied on in conduct of the business should be listed as being transferred from seller to buyer. It's useful for a copy of each of these documents to be included with the offer, and then attached once the offer becomes the purchase contract.*

❖ *Among the seller agreements that become part of the finished contract are the pledge to train the buyer in the business and the non-compete covenant, which will extend for a period of months or years beyond close of escrow as agreed on by the buyer and seller.*

❖ *The chief buyer agreement in a transaction – beyond dealing in good faith – is to honor the non-disclosure/confidentiality agreement until the end of the transaction.*

❖ *Hard to measure or value, the goodwill of a company being purchased is probably the most important asset the buyer will acquire. In most situations, the goodwill includes the customer list, although there are industries in which it is treated as a separate asset.*

❖ *Buyer and seller are required by the Internal Revenue Service (IRS) to include an allocation of the purchase price in the purchase agreement. The allocation includes a specific value for each asset, and those values will be reflected in the tax returns of the parties to the transaction. For example, the value for depreciable assets will be shown in the buyer's return because of the depreciation that will be claimed. In the seller's return, the value of these assets will be compared to the value shown in prior returns so a determination can be made whether the seller gained or lost money by the sale of these assets, and whether or not a capital gains tax is due.*

❖ *The seller's representations and warranties refer to the viability of the business and the truth and accuracy of any statements about it that were made by the seller. The buyer's representations have to do with his or her ability to perform according to the contract.*

❖ *The purchase agreement states what the buyer expects to purchase. Also mentioned is that all assets are free and clear of liens or encumbrances. The buyer may choose to accept the business subject to (that is, along with) the claims against its assets, and/or take on some of the debt. In that event, the purchase price would be reduced by the amount.*

❖ *The seller ordinarily pays off all payables owed to vendors by the business and collects the receivables due to the business. Variations on this arrangement are possible if parties arrange for the buyer to collect receivables and/or pay payables.*

CHAPTER THIRTEEN

NEGOTIATING FOR WHAT YOU WANT

Children are admonished by their parents, after a trip to the circus, not to try and mimic the dangerous stunts they saw performed by professionals.

I won't give you the same advice about representing yourself when negotiating to purchase a small California business – for one thing, you can't break any bones by failing to execute a move properly, while discussing a deal. But if you're inexperienced at reaching an agreement while balancing between what you need, and what the other party is trying to achieve, it could be hazardous to your financial health to do this yourself.

If you have a competent broker or agent working with you, it's best to leave the negotiating up to him or to her. And your job is to let the representative know what you want and what you won't accept.

Even with professional help, it doesn't hurt for you to know some of the basic ideas behind intelligent negotiating. You might find you have a gift for it, and your input will be helpful in establishing a workable package of price and terms.

Here are some of the ideas which help guide skilled negotiators.

Don't Take it Personally

You should know, for instance, that there's little room for emotions when talking about your money. For some people, of course, the fear of loss or the anticipation of gain can evoke strong feelings, and these get revealed in a display of one kind or another. But it's best if you can control the outward signs of your anger, elation, sadness, frustration or whatever you are feeling when your proposals are rejected, or even when your suggestions are adopted, as you conduct discussions with the seller of a business you'd like to buy.

The necessity of separating emotions from business should seem obvious. And yet I have seen intelligent, successful business people who react as if they or their ideas are being criticized severely, when a seller explains the reasons for not wanting to accept an offer.

Can you separate your business dealings from the emotional investment you've made in your campaign to buy a company? Your outbursts may aggravate, scare, intimidate or even please the people sitting on the other side of the table. But it's unlikely the seller will change his or her mind about something because of your behavior. And if you are able to keep your feelings in check, you'll come across as a more powerful figure – someone to be reckoned with – and that can help you get some of the concessions you want.

Besides, you'll be able to manage your side of the negotiations from strength, rather than feel vulnerable, victimized and a little scared.

Remain Focused on Your Objective

When you're in the middle of a battle about a particular subject, don't lose sight of what you're trying to accomplish. With a clear objective that you keep in your head – a vision of a completed deal to work for – you're less likely to find yourself heavily engaged in a battle over matters that are much less consequential than your goal. Don't allow yourself to be distracted. And don't fix on a particular issue that's relatively unimportant to you, compared to the accomplishment of the overall objective.

That means, for example that you'll recognize the value of a "bird in hand."

Indeed, a seller may be quite difficult to deal with. And you may feel yourself being pushed toward your limits of patience as well as to the edge of your willingness to negotiate. But are you sure you'd be better off starting from scratch? What if it takes awhile to find another suitable business? What if the next seller isn't any easier to work with than this one?

Consider this: You've devoted a great deal of time and money – taken on the hard work, endured the difficult circumstances and maintained patience during the long process – so that you could find a great business and get a fair deal that will enable you to become a business owner. Let that be your mantra when you encounter issues that threaten to derail negotiations for the company you want to buy.

You may be making a mistake if you stick stubbornly to a minor issue without being mindful of its overall impact on the deal.

Importance of Flexibility

Certainly, there are matters about which you need to be firm. Some parts of your offering are critical to the overall deal, and it might not make sense to enter into a transaction if your most important needs are neglected. But be selective about what provisions are true deal killers and which are not.

Is it possible you can consider the seller's request for a different payoff period than you'd anticipated? Or for a higher interest rate than you'd planned? These need not be deal killers if there's a way you can accommodate the seller and keep the transaction on track without seriously damaging your cash flow planning.

I've heard a number of stories over the years from business brokers and agents about how their clients became stubborn, rather unnecessarily, over relatively minor matters, and then realized, later on, that they might have had a good deal, had they been a bit more open to other ideas. These are disappointed buyers who learned, the hard way, that flexibility is an important attribute when you're negotiating to purchase a business.

Starting from the Bottom Line

If you know the absolute highest price to which you'll agree, as well as the point at which the terms of purchase would be unacceptable, you're prepared to enter into negotiations. Assuming that you and a seller are far apart regarding some of the provisions of the contract for your purchase of a business, you can let the other party know that you feel it's worth exploring how a compromise can be reached. It means each of you must be willing to give a little. If you get agreement on this point, it means the other person is willing to try and work out a deal, and will renegotiate where possible.

From that point it's just a matter of discussing each of the issues, perhaps moving back and forth among them – you get a provision important to you, the seller gets his or her terms on another aspect – until either a final agreement is achieved, or it becomes clear that there can't be a deal without moving beyond the bottom line that one or both of you has established.

For example, if you are unwilling, under any circumstances, to pay more than $200,000 for the business, and the seller insists that the least she'll accept is $230,000, it's not worth your time to continue discussing the matter. But if the seller says "I'd only agree to $200,000 if I had excellent terms," that might be an opening to continue negotiating.

Suppose you comply with the seller's strict payoff schedule on the portion of the purchase price being carried back, and you also agreed to pay a higher interest rate than you'd planned. This is the time to let the seller know that since you have given in on the last couple of items, you'd like her to agree to an extended period of training. This will allow you to conserve some of the working capital you would have used for extra payroll, and will increase the probability that you'll be successful in the business.

The value of this style of negotiating is that it recognizes each party has a bottom line that can't be violated, though you don't reveal your positions. You agree to respect each others' thresholds, to end negotiations if a deal can't be struck within the parameters acceptable to each of you.

But every thing else is fair game, as you work to find some combination of give and take that can lead you to an agreement.

Building from Consensus

Another approach is to explore the issues with the seller about which you can agree. If you see eye-to-eye about the terms of the deal, the covenant not to compete, and other factors, you can isolate just those few points on which you do not agree. Then you can chip away at those bones of contention, either by meeting somewhere in the middle, or by taking turns granting a concession. Or both.

I've watched skilled negotiators use this technique very effectively. Sometimes when parties to a transaction in progress reach an impasse, someone will say:

"Let's review again the items that we DO agree on. " The object of this exercise, of course, is to concentrate on the positive aspects of your agreement – the areas where you are in concurrence – as a motivation to find a solution for the negotiating points not yet resolved.

Take a Time Out

Experienced negotiators also know the value of postponing further discussion if opposing parties are getting nowhere in their talks. Rather than arriving at the conclusion that there is no way a deal can be struck, why not reconvene in an hour, or in a few days, when tempers have cooled and principals have had a chance to think through their needs and objectives? A buyer and seller may be able to come back after rethinking their positions and work out a satisfactory deal with provisions they couldn't see clearly in the heat of negotiations, before the break.

Of course, the choice to separate temporarily, for a cooling off period, can work to the detriment of an agreement. It's possible, during the time between negotiating sessions, that one or both of the participants will decide they are not willing to continue negotiating with the other person along the same lines

In either event, the choice to "cool it" for awhile, usually gives people the opportunity to gain some perspective on the issues at hand, so each can determine what is in his or her best interests.

If you and the seller of a business you want to purchase find yourselves spinning your negotiating wheels and not making progress, perhaps a time out is the best choice.

Conclusion

It's easy to get distracted in the middle of negotiations for the purchase of a small California business, and to believe that the seller is trying to take advantage of you. But if you try on some of the ideas proposed here, you may be able to see the situation in less threatening terms. And that may help you to continue to engage in negotiations until you arrive at a deal that allows you to buy the business along the lines of – if not blissful ecstasy – at least, terms you can live with.

KEY POINTS FROM THIS CHAPTER

❖ *Considering that you, the buyer of a small California business, and most any seller have contradictory objectives, it can be very difficult to negotiate an agreement. And this challenge is compounded in situations in which buyers are their own representatives, not able to benefit from the services of an objective intermediary who can sometimes work out these differences between parties.*

❖ *It's useful to try and keep your emotions in check when talking business. It is understandable that people have strong feelings when their fortunes are at stake in their discussions, but showing anger, frustration, even elation, makes it harder to maintain the "cool head" needed to arrive at intelligent decisions in difficult negotiations. A seller's desire to receive more money than you want to pay for a business need not be interpreted as a criticism about you or your business style.*

❖ *By remembering the overall objective – to buy the business at workable terms – can help to prevent obsessing about details of a transaction that, in the long run, are not critically important.*

❖ *However, buyers are not urged to agree to provisions that are contrary to their best interests. To decide what is and is not in your best interests, requires that you look at the transaction as a whole and consider long and short-term costs as well as gains.*

❖ *One way to bring parties together on an agreement is for each to determine their bottom line for every issue – the full extent to which they will agree regarding price, terms, and the other components of a buy/sell contract. Then try to compromise on terms in a way that these bottom lines aren't crossed.*

❖ *Another negotiating strategy to achieve a deal is to start with agreement on every item about which parties are in accord. Then build on this success by trying to reach a fair consensus on the other issues, one by one. Sometimes if there are two problem areas, the resolution is for one party to win on one, the other party gets the second.*

❖ *A timeout is an excellent way for people to clear their heads from the intense, stressful experience of negotiating a business deal. Once they've had a chance to gain a broader perspective it may be easier to reach agreement or, alternatively, to see that there is no likelihood of agreement.*

CHAPTER FOURTEEN

THE DEAL

In the preceding chapters, I've endeavored to offer anyone interested in buying a small California business some ideas about narrowing your focus, preparing for the search, finding available opportunities, determining what to pay, and negotiating for your terms. The culmination of all your efforts to date is represented by the purchase agreement. This document, which is likely to be the same form used for the offer, articulates the provisions by which you and the seller are prepared to complete your transaction – the blueprint for your business arrangement. And it is the definitive record, if needed in the future, of the deal by which you became the owner of your business.

At this point it will be helpful for you to know what items should be covered by your agreement, and you may want a suggestion about whether you want to hire an attorney to prepare it. I'll address this last question first.

Using Your attorney

As a general rule, I suggest relying on a broker – if one is involved in the transaction – to draft the purchase agreement. An experienced business sales professional knows what provisions to include and is familiar with the language to use when describing components of standard agreements. Your attorney can then be called on to review the document and let you know if there are any parts of the contract which leave you at risk of exposure to potential legal or financial trouble.

Your attorney may not agree with this advice. Most legal representatives like to be called in at the beginning, before ink meets paper, so they have a hand in creating the deal, rather than just looking it over to make sure you're adequately protected. And if yours is a particularly complicated transaction, involving the transfer of corporate stock and requiring a number of warranties and other unusual provisions, a lawyer-drafted contract might be advisable. But most sales of small California businesses involve the transfer of assets, not stock, and the particulars of the agreements can be adequately described using one of the forms available from several sources for this purpose.

You'll save several hundred dollars by drafting your own agreement, and it's easy to insure your protection by including a contingency that states you are able to back out of the agreement if it does not meet the approval of your attorney, who will look at it afterward.

Then you can run the contract past your legal representative who will charge you for an hour or two of his or her time reviewing the agreement and discussing it with you – letting you know about any concerns and how to address them. By contrast, if the attorney is called on to prepare a purchase agreement from scratch, it will involve meeting with you and with the seller, and racking up a total of several hours billable time.

If you have experience working with an attorney on a business problem, you may be aware that once you have an attorney, the other side – in this case the seller – will feel it's important to be represented in the same way. That means your attorney-written contract will go to the seller's legal representative, and it will come back with modifications, necessitating another trip to your attorney's office and a few more hours for which you'll have to pay.

Aside from the expense, there is the risk that if attorneys get involved early in a deal, they may load negotiations with so many provisions and protections – so many mentions of whereas and wherefore – that you and the seller might actually become discouraged about the idea of going forward with your deal.

I know of potential transactions that never worked because the momentum for a deal was dissipated in the weeks during which the legal gears ground slowly and laboriously. It became too costly and too complicated for the principles to continue to work for a transaction while their attorneys wrestled over a seemingly endless list of legal issues having little to do with completing the transaction.

You can save yourself these problems if all of the necessary provisions for the sale are included in the offer you presented to the seller. And once signed, it can readily serve as your agreement.

Alternatively, you can put the broker to work, drafting a contract that reflects the agreements contained in the offer. Another option, if you and the seller prefer the do-it-yourself style of entrepreneurship, is to just access one of the forms that work perfectly well for most small California business transactions. You'll find one at *www.bizben.com* Select the "Forms" button, then open and download the Conditional Purchase and Sale of Assets Agreement.

What's Included in the Purchase Agreement-Basic Provisions

Following is a reminder of some of the items that belong in your contract. And as 90% of the purchases of small California businesses involve business assets, rather than corporate stock, I'll confine the discussion to the more common type of transaction.

Starting with the basics, the contract you'll use to buy a business will first note the date and identify you as the purchaser, and will include the name and address of the subject business, and name of the seller. Then it will state the purchase price and detail how it is to be paid. The amount of down payment is noted, then terms of payoff are spelled out, with an exact description of the note structure. For example, if the seller is carrying back a portion of the purchase price, does the note call for regular monthly payments over a specified time, one or more balloon payments, a delay of payments, or months when payments may be skipped? This is explained in detail in the agreement so the instructions are clear for the escrow holder, who will be charged with the responsibility of drafting the note, or the notes – if there are more than one.

If additional financing is required to complete the transaction, that should be addressed as the next subject in the contact. And it's important to make clear whether obtaining financing is a requirement for the transaction to be completed – that is, a contingency in the deal. The agreement can even specify the finance terms that are acceptable to you, with respect to length of payoff and interest rate charged, so there is no question as to what will be required to remove this contingency.

The escrow holder also will need specific instructions about collateralizing any notes. Will the business assets provide the security? Have you and the seller agreed on other collateral, such as your personal or real property, to back up the obligation? Details about this part of the agreement need to be included in the contract, with the discussion about the promissory notes.

The lease and franchise rights

Determination of the leasehold interest belonging to the business is usually treated as the next item in the agreement. Will the lease be transferred as is? Is there a contingency regarding your ability to obtain the lease at the same terms? Is a new lease required as part of the deal?

If you are purchasing a franchise business, there should be mention of how the transfer is to be handled. It's likely that the contract form will be supplied by the franchisor. In fact the franchisor may be able to act as the escrow holder (or may insist on it). Determine if you, or the seller, or both, will pay for franchise transfer fees, if any. Some franchise owners don't get assistance from the franchisor when it comes to selling. If that includes the business you are buying, it might be necessary to include franchisor approval of the transfer as a contingency.

Capital assets

What follows in the agreement is the detail of items included in the sale. As this text is concerned with the asset sale, I recommend that the individual items be specifically noted, usually on a separate list. Such list should cover all capital equipment, including vehicles, if there are trucks or cars belonging to the business and part of the sale.

Typically the leasehold improvements are included as assets. They may be given a value in the transaction and are used by the owner of the business, and yet these items ultimately might be written off the business books if they are attached to the real estate and belong to the landlord. Leases ordinarily stipulate whether title to leasehold improvements stays with the owner of the real property or with the tenant who owns the business. These improvements in a restaurant, for example, can include the stoves, ranges, hoods, counters, sinks, dishwasher, built-in refrigeration and other fixtures attached to the real property and used by the restaurant owner. In the interest of avoiding disputes, it's best if the lease clearly designates the ownership of trade fixtures that are considered leasehold improvements. That provision within the lease can be referenced in the purchase agreement so you and the seller are clear about what is included in the sale.

Inventory

Treatment of inventory – how much is anticipated at cost, at close of escrow, and whether it is to be included as part of the purchase price – is a subject that needs to be addressed in the contract. If the purchase price includes inventory of parts, supplies and materials, the actual sale price will be adjusted at the closing, by the variation in value of inventory – when it is counted and computed – from the projected amount.

For example, a sale price fixed at $100,000.00 that assumes a $20,000.00 inventory value, may be increased to, say $102,000.00 if the physical count of inventory reveals a total amount of $22,000.00 at cost. Conversely, you may get the business for $98,700.00 if the total dollar amount representing inventory is counted and computed at $18,700.00. With brokers involved in a transaction, and a commission based on total price, the principals usually are encouraged by their broker representatives to include inventory as part of the deal. Inventory inclusion boosts the business sales price, and hence the commission. You and the seller, however, should handle the inventory in whatever way you deem easier and more appropriate to the circumstances.

The opposite approach, which may save the seller a bit of commission, is to have the purchase price include all assets of the business, except inventory. If inventory is paid for in addition to the business, this fact needs to be made clear in the agreement. It is useful here to specify an estimated figure so the escrow holder has an idea of about how much to charge you for inventory once it's counted. Also, don't forget to specify whether the inventory amount is to be added to cash collected from you at close of escrow or added to the promissory note that represents your obligation to the seller.

Employment agreements

It is likely that as part of the deal, you have agreed that the seller will be "employed" by the company for a period of time following the close. In most cases, this does not mean he or she is added to the payroll, but will take on the assignment of introducing you to customers, suppliers and other individuals important to the functioning of the company. And the seller will train you in the operation of the business. The terms of this understanding should be noted, as they will be incorporated into a training agreement, prepared by the escrow and presented to you and the seller for signature at the close. Depending on what you've worked out with the seller, the training contract may require the seller's involvement during some hours at the place of business, or require the seller to be available by phone for consultation, or both. Usually, the training period is defined in terms of the number of days or weeks that it extends beyond the close.

The other common form of employment contract is the covenant not to compete, in which your seller agrees not to be active as a principal, employee or contractor for any firm engaged in the same business as the one you are buying. This agreement also has a specified period after which it expires, usually coinciding with the length of time provided for paying off the promissory note – say, three or five years. Thus, when you're finished paying the seller, the seller will no longer be required to refrain from competing with your business. There should be a geographic definition for the covenant, setting the number of miles from the subject business in which the seller is not allowed to compete or work for a competitor. The terms then of this agreement will be incorporated into the covenant not to compete which, like the training agreement, will be presented to you and the seller for approval at close of escrow.

What's Included in the Purchase Agreement-Special Provisions

Are there any additional agreements made part of your contract to deal with special problems? Suppose, for example, that you fear the loss of business if a major customer – rumored to be moving from the area – does relocate soon after close, and the company (when it belongs to you) loses the customer's business. If the seller – in order to reach an agreement with you – said he would compensate you for part of this loss – provided that move occurs – the exact understanding about this matter needs to be included in the purchase agreement. Most likely, the precise terms of this understanding, including the way to determine the compensation and how it is paid (in cash, deducted from note or by some other means) will be reduced to writing in the form of an addendum in escrow. This will be among the papers you and the seller will sign at the close. And if action taken under this provision will impact the terms of the promissory note, the note should be prepared so as to recognize the special agreement. It might refer to the agreement and include language that explains how the terms of the note are to be altered in the event the provision is enacted.

Items excluded

In many cases, there are items which are present in the place of business that are not included in the deal. It may be sufficient for you and the seller to agree to a standard provision in your contract which states that anything not on the list of assets transferred is deemed to be excluded from the sale.

But it doesn't hurt to create a separate list of excluded items for inclusion in the contract, so there is no confusion or misunderstanding about what is and is not to belong to you at the close.

Understood to be excluded from an asset sale are items that belong on the balance sheet of the business. It's unlikely that you have agreed to take such seller assets as the cash on hand. Receivables usually remain with the seller and technically, it is his or her responsibility to collect them, even after the close. It's not uncommon, however, if receivables come in – for example, to a retail store – for you to collect money owed to the company (actually belonging to the former owner) while you're conducting the normal course of business. Then you would turn the collections on the receivables over to the seller. Naturally, it's important to keep good records so both parties know who is entitled to which funds.

An alternate plan is for you to purchase the receivables at a discount (commonly between 50% and 80% of their face value), in which event you'll keep all money coming in, even those funds paying for business conducted before the transfer of ownership.

Items on the other side of the balance sheet ordinarily stay with the seller as well. Long term debt should be paid off or otherwise handled by the seller so any capital assets you receive will be transferred free of encumbrances. Additionally, the payables are deemed to belong to the seller unless there is a specific provision in the agreement to the contrary.

And any special arrangements you've worked out with your seller regarding long or short term debt should be clearly explained in the contract and will likely be incorporated into addenda, promissory notes, and/or other documents included for approval with the closing papers.

Some deals use the assumption of obligations by the buyer as a way of reducing cash requirements to close escrow. If, for example, the seller owes $30,000.00 in trade payables, the buyer may decide that by assuming these obligation and paying them off in 90 days, he or she can hold back that amount of cash, using it to promote the business growth, rather than including the funds as part of the down payment. The seller, in other words, will receive $30,000 less at close, but will not have the $30,000 obligation that was originally anticipated. The sum due to suppliers ultimately is paid from income earned by the business. In effect, the buyer arranged for a 90-day loan (usually at low interest). This is likely to be okay with a seller who had planned to use that money to eliminate the $30,000.00 short term debt at the close. Of course, it's necessary to get the approval of the creditors – suppliers and providers of service to the business, who are owed the $30,000. If this strategy is followed, the contract and the closing instructions must specify that the buyer, in taking over the business, is assuming the $30,000 obligation that was incurred prior to the transfer of ownership

Contingencies

After laying out the parts of your agreement, noting what is being sold and for how much, the contract deals with the procedures needed for the transaction to be completed.

Just as the buyer and seller in the transaction for a home rely on contingencies to protect themselves from having to perform until all the required actions are completed and the facts are in, you and your seller are waiting for certain things to take place before you move forward. It is the contingencies part of your agreement which outlines the work you both have to do and describes what has to be satisfactorily resolved in order for the transaction to proceed to the next step. We already have touched on a number of these contingencies. They cover the transfer or rewriting of the lease, the franchisor accepting you as its new franchisee (if that is applicable), your satisfactory review of the business books and records, your ability to obtain a certain amount of financing and also the satisfactory inspection and review, by you, of any other issues that pertain to the viability of the business.

As suggested above, the approval of your attorney regarding the content and wording of the agreement, also can be made a contingency.

Any other conditions which must be satisfied before you will proceed would be noted here. The seller's contingencies also should be included at this point. The agreement might give him or her the right to make sure you have the financial condition you stated, and that you are a suitable and qualified buyer, before proceeding.

When all contingencies, on behalf of both parties, have been made a part of this section of the agreement, it's a good idea to review them, making sure the explanations are clear and complete. It's important that you and the seller both know exactly what needs to take place to have a deal, and what might prevent moving forward.

Unlike other components of the transaction, however, the contingencies are not usually included in the escrow papers, for the reason that these items should have been resolved prior to getting into escrow, and are no longer at issue at that point.

As noted earlier, your time limit to review the business records and remove this contingency should be brief enough to keep things moving forward at a steady pace. While seven to ten business days is a usual time frame for the buyer's conduct of due diligence, there may be delays if you are waiting for the landlord's participation so you can verify that the lease will be satisfactorily transferred or that a new lease, acceptable to you, will be granted. If you're dependent on a lender because of a financing contingency, there also may be a delay past your seven to ten day deadline while the money sources cross their "T"s, dot their "I"s, and determine if and when the cash will be forthcoming.

If you took the time beforehand, to work on pre-approval by a lender, you may reap the reward with a quick okay when it comes time to handle the financing contingency.

Despite the best planning, of course, there may be delays which remain out of your control. That's when it's a good idea to make certain you and the seller remain in contract. You each can sign a separate note or jointly approve an addendum that refers to the contract and stipulates that you're both in accord about the likely delay and about a new deadline for contingency removal. Otherwise, you technically would be out of contract. If the seller wanted to change his or her mind, perhaps accept another offer, there may be grounds to do so if the specified period has passed without written removal of the contingencies.

And what about the seller's contingency removal? He or she may need some time – the same seven to ten days is recommended – to verify your creditworthiness. After all, the seller may soon be accepting your note for part of the purchase price when turning the business over to you.

What's Included in the Purchase Agreement-Escrow and Legal Provisions

At this point in the agreement, you and the seller can include the name and address of the escrow holder, and set out a plan for you to deliver, to escrow, your deposit check – the one that was presented to the seller with the offer. It's customary for the buyer to increase the deposit when opening escrow and this provision should be included in your agreement. Also, determine who will pay for escrow services. They start at about $1,000 to $10,000 (depending on size of transaction) for the most basic of escrows, including fees and charges for the preparation of other documents and for the work needed to comply with the law and complete your transaction. Local business brokers can make recommendations as to competent escrow holders and you can find some able escrow services in the resources section at *www.bizben.com* While the question of who pays this cost is sometimes determined with further negotiations between buyer and seller, the parties usually make the choice to split the escrow expenses, and this is recommended as the easiest way to resolve the matter. If you're in the mood to do a little more wheeling and dealing, you can use this point as a bargaining chip. If, during negotiations, the seller is resisting an idea that's important to you, perhaps you can prevail by offering to pay all escrow fees if the other party will go along with you on that point. Alternatively, when it comes time to insert into your agreement who will pay for the escrow service, you may want to remind the seller of your last concession during the negotiations, and then announce: "you owe me one," suggesting that the other party pick up the escrow's bill.

The date for closing the deal should be the next entry into your contract. Don't forget the ticking of the clock that will occur while the work is being done to remove contingencies. That should be completed and contingencies removed before escrow is opened. And then there is a roughly two week period during which time the escrow is opened, the notice of bulk transfer is published (more about this later), and the 12 business day "window" required by the State of California, is open for any creditors of the business to submit their claims. Keeping these time consuming projects in mind, you can refer to your calendar and decide when you and the seller can schedule the transfer to take place.

We'll cover the escrow time requirement in a bit more detail in subsequent pages. For now it's important that you realize even an accepted offer may require a month or so to mature into a closed transaction. This is particularly useful to keep in mind if you're attempting to close a deal before a specific time. More than one buyer who failed to allow enough closing time was surprised and disappointed to learn that a deal would drag over into the following calendar year and disrupt the buyer's careful tax planning.

The legal provisions

The final paragraphs of your buy/sell agreement will likely include some of the language that lawyers have added over the years, meant to clarify issues and install procedures that can help keep you and other small California business sellers and buyers out of court.

The representations and warranties wording that should go in at this point in the contract, make it clear that the buyer will fully investigate the business and will purchase it only if satisfied as a result of that investigation. The idea here is to protect the seller from someone who has buyer's remorse and claims to have been somehow forced, coerced or tricked into making the purchase. A common provision, usually added here, is that if the buyer can't or won't put up the rest of the money after removing contingencies, or fails to perform in other respects, the buyer's deposit money, sitting in escrow, will be considered liquidated damages and will be paid to the seller to compensate him or her for time and trouble.

There also are some protections for the buyer that belong in this section of the contract. They include the seller's representations to the effect that he or she is not aware of any conditions or circumstances that will negatively impact the business. If the seller has learned of a competitor moving into the area, or some other factor that would impact the business, that fact should have been revealed to you – preferably in writing. If it was not, and the factor later proves to hurt your business, you may have legal standing to seek remedies by suing the seller for misrepresentation, or concealing material information.

A similar declaration from the seller refers to the condition of the equipment – that it is in good working order, and the inventory – that it is merchantable. In other words, the seller is not aware of any reason that the inventory would be rejected by customers as too old, out-of-date or otherwise undesirable.

There also may be some language which addresses the possibility of a dispute and provides for the means of settling it – by arbitration, if possible, rather than a lawsuit. And as noted earlier in this chapter, you can run the contract past your attorney for recommendations as to other legal protections that belong in this part of the agreement.

Conclusion

The purchase agreement that you and the seller work out, after you've completed your negotiations, provides the blue print for your acquisition of the business. The agreement reviews the details – the price, terms, and allocation – for your transaction. And it lists precisely what is and what is not included in the transaction. The contingencies are noted along with the time in which they are to be removed. An escrow company should be named and you and the buyer will be prepared to take the buyer's check to open an escrow as soon as the due diligence process is completed.

KEY POINTS FROM THIS CHAPTER

❖ *Having reached accord with the seller on your acquisition of a small California business, you now will begin to complete the deal by drafting and signing the purchase agreement. The contract may be the form you used to make the offer, or you and the seller might prefer to draft a new contract, incorporating the points listed in the offer.*

❖ *Buyers are advised to use the broker, if one is involved, to prepare your contract. If you and the seller are working without benefit of a knowledgeable third party, you can write up the deal yourselves, using one of the forms available for this purpose. This is a preferable approach to hiring an attorney to draft your agreement.*

❖ *Not only will you save hundreds, perhaps thousands of dollars by drafting your own agreement, you also will prevent the possibility of having to deal with a long, unwieldy document – the frequent result when attorneys take over the assignment.*

❖ *Your attorney's agreement with the language and content of your contract can be made a contingency of the contract, so that you get the legal protection you want.*

❖ *Some 90% of small California business sales involve the transfer of business assets, as distinct from corporate stock sales. This review focuses on the more common type of transaction.*

❖ *A sample purchase/sale agreement can be viewed and downloaded by visiting www.bizben.com/selling-buying-business-forms.php Click on Conditional Purchase and Sale of Assets Agreement.*

❖ *The purchase agreement begins by noting the date and identifying the purchaser and the business. That's followed with a description of agreed-on price and terms, including allocation of the price.*

❖ *Seller financing should be explained in detail so that parties are clear about what was agreed, and so that escrow has explicit instructions for preparation of needed documents, such as any promissory notes.*

❖ *At some point in the agreement it is important to add a description of the contingencies related to financing and to an acceptable lease.*

❖ *A clear statement of what is included in the sale – a complete list of capital assets is recommended – should be part of your contract. Following that is the statement of parties' agreement regarding the inventory – will a certain amount (at cost) be included in the sale price or considered an addition to the price?*

❖ *Employment contracts in the agreement usually refer to the seller's obligation to train the buyer – with specifics about where and for how long that will take place – and to not compete with the buyer's new business for a specified period of time in a defined geographic area. The covenant not to compete is often timed to expire when the buyer's obligation to the seller – if the seller is financing part of the purchase price – is paid in full.*

❖ *Any special arrangements or understandings agreed on by parties should be explained in detail so there is no confusion about this part of the deal, and so that the escrow holder is equipped to prepare any supporting documents necessitated by such agreements.*

❖ *Any items at the business premises but not to be included in the business sale, should be listed and approved by buyer and seller so there is no misunderstanding on this point.*

❖ *While the business receivables, generated prior to the sale, are kept by the seller, it is not uncommon for the buyer to collect them on behalf of the seller, or to buy them at a discount.*

❖ *Sellers expect to pay off the company's short term and long term debt and turn over the business free and clear of obligation. However, if the buyer agrees to assume some of the debt – and that's okay with the creditor – it can help to reduce the amount of cash needed to close escrow. Frequently the buyer can use the money to improve the business.*

❖ *Any contingencies agreed on by the parties, that need to be satisfied and removed prior to opening escrow, should be specified in the sales contract. Contingencies probably include you being able to obtain the premises lease and being satisfied with a review of the business books, records and other information. And the seller may make the deal contingent on being satisfied after a review of your financial standing and credit worthiness.*

❖ *Franchise business owners may find the franchisor has provided all the resources needed to establish a deal and conduct escrow. If not, your contract with the buyer should be contingent on franchisor approval of the sale.*

❖ *The agreement then takes up the matter of escrow: Who will conduct the escrow, what the escrow will be required to do and who will pay the escrow fees? A 50/50 split of escrow costs between buyer and seller is a common practice.*

❖ *An anticipated closing date is noted, after parties add in the time that will be needed in order to comply with California's legal requirements for a bulk transfer of business property.*

❖ *Toward the end of the agreement, buyers and sellers add their representations and warranties to provide protection for each other. You acknowledge that you will conduct due diligence and rely on those findings to decide whether to go forward with the purchase. The seller warrants that equipment is in good, working order, the inventory is merchantable, and that there are no factors, known and undisclosed to the buyer, which might affect the fortunes of the business. Buyers often agree that if they fail to complete the transaction after removal of contingencies, their seller will be allowed to collect the buyer's money on deposit as liquidated damages.*

❖ *There may be delays in the process as buyer and seller are relying on others – lenders and landlord, for example – to be involved in the work of removing contingencies. It is useful for the principles in the transaction to agree in writing to any extensions of the deadlines, necessitated by these delays, in order to remain "in contract."*

YOU'VE GOT AN AGREEMENT. NOW WHAT?

Your dreams of being in business for yourself are coming closer if you have a purchase agreement that's ratified (signed by you and by the seller). It hasn't quite happened yet. You haven't taken over. And there are some very critical steps that need to be taken – projects you must complete – before the business is yours.

Why Half the Deals Fail

Incidentally, you should be aware that half of the signed purchase agreements on small businesses in California never go through. That means, statistically, you have a 50/50 chance of actually buying the business that has occupied your time and attention as you've spent days or even weeks learning about the company, considering various options and then negotiating for its purchase.

The key reason that deals fail at this point – when the buyers are conducting careful analysis of the subject business following a signed purchase agreement – is that the businesses don't meet the buyers' expectations. Too often, the person or company that the buyer must rely on for the premises lease transfer or the granting of franchise rights is unwilling to cooperate. And this frequently comes after the seller has assured the buyer that there will be "no problem" about getting these third party approvals!

Whether the seller was misinformed about what would happen, or felt that he or she could persuade this critical third party to cooperate, the buyer's time has been wasted, the hopes were needlessly raised, and it will be necessary to start the hunt all over again. The inability to get the needed approval from the landlord, the franchisor or some other third party without whom the buyer can't proceed, is a deal killer. It's time to go back to square one.

The other unmet expectation that destroys a deal has to do with the performance of the business, and the comparison the buyer makes during the due diligence period, between the actual revenue figures presented for inspection and the statements about the revenues made by the seller or the broker or agent, when the buyer was getting acquainted with the company.

There have been circumstances I've witnessed where the business, when subjected to a due diligence examination, proved to be doing even better than the seller said. And that's a happy surprise. But in most cases that's not what happens.

I'm reminded of a young man – Larry – who worked in bicycle shops from the time he was in high school, dreaming of one day owning his own. He had definite plans for what he wanted to do – what products he wanted to offer, what repair services he wanted to feature and how he wanted to promote the business. He'd been disappointed when the bicycle store in which he worked, and thought he could buy, was sold to the owner's relative instead.

Larry then launched a campaign to find a store he could buy with the money he'd saved and a cash gift promised by his grandmother. After a few months he entered into a deal for a long established bicycle retail and repair business in a Southern California beach town and was nearly ecstatic about the impending close of escrow. He had just enough money for the required down payment and he would then make payments for the balance to the seller out of his earnings from the business.

During the due diligence examination, however, Larry was disappointed to notice that the shop's tax returns and bank statements told a different story about the revenues and earnings than did the seller when they first had talked.

When Larry pointed out the discrepancies, the seller's answer was that since Larry was not an accountant, he was not qualified to understand the business records. So Larry hired an accountant who reviewed the same information and came to the same conclusion.

Larry did not know what to do. He really wanted to buy the shop, but the accountant told him that it was not generating enough income to allow for the payments to the seller and for an income. Was Larry willing to work for free for a couple of years?

In their final conversation, the seller told Larry that it was only the checks and credit card receipts which were noted in the business records. All of the cash transactions were "off the books." The seller encouraged Larry to go through with the deal, assuring him that he'd make enough money.

Since the due diligence examination of the business records was a contingency of their agreement, Larry could back out of the deal if he wasn't satisfied. He spent a sleepless night debating with himself about the correct action.

Larry made the decision to ask for his deposit back and to continue looking for a bicycle business to buy, he hoped it would be from someone more forthright than the last seller with whom he'd dealt.

While it's usually a problem with the business that causes deals to fail before completion, there also are instances in which a buyer has tried to take on more than he or she can handle financially. If the bank won't come up with the needed funds to help the buyer close escrow, the likely result will be no deal. That is also the case if the seller conducts due diligence on the buyer's financial strength and is not comfortable with the findings.

What you can conclude from these observations is that if you have done a good job of preparing for your purchase – if you have the cash you'll need to complete the deal, with something left over for working capital, and if your credit history will stand up to inspection – then it's up to the seller to provide you what was promised, in the way of approvals and in the proof of the company's performance, in order for you to complete your purchase.

And while you hope everything will work out as you'd anticipated, it's a good idea not to start printing the company's new stationery just yet. Don't allow your enthusiasm to color your clear thinking. As much as you like and trust the seller, make sure that whatever information you are provided as part of your due diligence investigation is consistent with your expectations. You don't want surprises at this point. Your agreement with the seller should include a contingency for your satisfactory review of the business financials and the other details you want to analyze. If the unexpected happens – the business does not prove to be as profitable or as trouble-free as you were led to believe – be prepared to exercise your right to decline moving forward on the deal.

In fact, I recommend to buyers that they keep one eye open for other opportunities, even as they are conducting due diligence on a small California business they plan to buy. The seller will likely be taking back-up offers in case you don't work out as the buyer. There's no reason you shouldn't be aware of other offerings while you're checking out the business you have on contract.

Using Your Accountant for Financial Due Diligence Analysis

To aid in your due diligence examination, you may want to engage the services of an accountant. The professional's job will be to review the financial records of the company you want to buy and determine if the broker and the seller told you the truth when they quoted the figures for the company's revenues and the owner's income. Some buyers feel they can handle this responsibility themselves. Their investigation will involve matching documentation of sales, such as customer invoices and cash register receipts, with bank deposits. And they will compare items in the expense ledger of the P & L with the check book and statements from suppliers.

Much of this work involves just the tedious application of simple math. And you may want to conduct it yourself, if you're seeking to save some money and are competent with figures. Be aware, though, that there are a number of accounting procedures and practices with which you may not be familiar. It's easy to get confused when items are credited to one account and a corresponding debit needs to be entered to maintain the "balance" in the company's balance sheet.

Besides, there are ways to make a company look more profitable than it really is. If you're not familiar with some of the more sophisticated accounting techniques, you might be well advised to pay the fee for a competent professional to go over the records for you. He or she will know what to look for and will spot inconsistencies by which the information is not complete and accurate. And if there are questions about how the seller keeps track of certain items and reports on various categories of income and expenses, your professional will be able to ferret out the needed information and understand what is going on.

I've observed how buyers conducting due diligence can become confused and intimidated when the seller's CPA responds to their questions with complicated technical explanations. No need for that if you're represented by another professional who can talk the same language.

Other Due Diligence Tasks

In addition to the books and records, of course, there are other items you will want to inspect and to learn about during your period of due diligence. I think it's a good idea to see samples of the company's promotion and advertising efforts, and check out the firm's handbook, if there is one. That will give you insight into the rules for employees and the standard practices that are followed in the company.

Ask the seller to disclose information on any lawsuits in which the business was involved during the past five years. It's not important to know about the particulars of a specific action, but I would be concerned if a company has a history of being sued or of having to go to court to collect its receivables.

The seller's concerns about confidentiality may make it difficult for you to spend much time at the premises during business hours, as that might alert employees that something is going on. If you can manage to drop by for a few minutes in the guise of a customer or as a vendor, be as observant as possible. Do the employees seem productive? Is the phone ringing? What's the mood of the place – energetic and active, or slow and somber?

I'm not an advocate of fabricating stories, even to accomplish your covert mission of checking out the business. So I think it's a better cover for you to be introduced as a possible investor or as a friend of the owner – both of which are somewhat factual, rather than coming into the place of business with some elaborate falsification about how you are auditing the books or conducting an insurance investigation.

A manufacturer's representative for consumer products lines in San Diego took a few prospective buyers of her business to meet some account contacts. The seller wasn't ready to tell her customers – mostly department store buyers – that she was selling the business, but didn't feel it would be right to make up some outrageous story. So clients were told the person accompanying the rep was a possible new employee for her company. Once a buyer was secured, following an accepted offer and then a completed escrow, the customers were told that the person was going to be taking over the businesses. The seller felt the approach was appropriate because it put her customers on notice that she was in the process of making some changes, without getting into the details of what was being changed – the company's ownership.

If you have not reviewed the business' existing contracts with customers or employees, insurance policies, vendor agreements or other documents relevant to the business you're planning to buy, this is the time to make sure you do so. If these agreements are transferred, you will be responsible to perform on them and you'll reap their benefits. It's best to find out what's involved and make sure you are in agreement with these arrangements.

This also is the time to learn what you can about the industry in which the company functions, and whether it is growing or declining. What are prospects for the future of the area in which the company is located? This is particularly important if your future business is a retail company that depends on locals with discretionary income for its survival.

Conclusion

In the final inspections and due diligence of the business you want to buy, you should be aware of the fact that half of the accepted offers on small California businesses do not result in successfully concluded transactions, frequently due to the buyer's discovery that the offering doesn't live up to the way it was advertised.

Prospective buyers are cautioned not to get overly excited about the new business until you're certain that what you're learning about it corresponds with what you were told about it.

With benefits and disadvantages to conducting the financial due diligence on a do-it-yourself basis, it helps if you have some skill and experience in analyzing company records. Otherwise, it's smart to bring in an accounting professional.

Other due diligence tasks include observing the business – though that can be difficult in light of the need for confidentiality – and studying agreements the company has with customers, employees and vendors.

KEY POINTS FROM THIS CHAPTER

❖ *You have a 50/50 chance, statistically, of successfully completing a purchase following an accepted offer. That's primarily because businesses don't always stand up to inspections, and because the approvals and clearances needed for change of ownership are not always forthcoming.*

❖ *While you don't have control over the circumstances of the business – it's up to the seller to relay all the facts, correctly, and be ready to support statements with proof – you can uphold your end of the agreement by making sure that you accurately represent your financial abilities.*

❖ *Just as a smart seller takes back up offers – even when there is a ratified deal in progress, you are well advised to keep looking at other opportunities as you go through due diligence review on a business you have a contract to buy.*

❖ *Engaging an accountant to conduct financial analysis on a company you are intending to purchase is probably the surest way to learn quickly if the company does enough profitable business to reward you for your efforts and to help retire the debt taken on to make the purchase.*

❖ *You may want to examine the books and records yourself, not working with an accountant, but the major benefit – saving the fee you would spend on the professional's work – may not be worth the risk of being misled about the financial performance of the company.*

❖ *Don't stop at financial information when conducting due diligent examination of a prospective business to buy. Make sure you view the contracts with employees, vendors and customers and other agreements important to the company's operation.*

❖ *Other things to inform yourself about while conducting due diligence on a company, are prior lawsuits, trends in the industry and changes in the geographic area where the company conducts business.*

CHAPTER SIXTEEN

THE WORKINGS OF ESCROW

If you remember the scenes from movies taking place in the Old West, you might recall that when two gamblers had a bet going they engaged a stakeholder to hang onto the cash that each put up and then pass the whole kitty over to the one who drew the most aces, or fired the most silver dollars out of the air with his six shooter, or whatever the bet. Or the middleman in a horse sale took responsibility for making sure that the seller showed up with the designated stallion and that the buyer brought all the money agreed on.

The job of stakeholder pretty much describes one of the key assignments of escrow companies hired to handle the documents and the money involved in the transfer of small California businesses in the 21st Century. But things have become a bit more complex since then, so the escrow holder has much more to do than just stuff the cash in one blue jeans' pocket and the business ownership certificate in the other.

And to make sure everyone knows what they're supposed to be doing, California legislators put together a fairly extensive set of rules for such business transactions – rules found in the State's Uniform Commercial code, mostly in Provisions 6102 through 6108.

You'll be glad to know that once you're dealing with the escrow company, much of your work is finally behind you. Ideally you don't open an escrow until contingencies have been removed. That means you are satisfied with everything reviewed during the due diligence examination, the landlord has agreed to cooperate with transfer of the lease or to establish new terms acceptable to you, the franchisor has "blessed" your deal (if the business is a franchise), and any lenders – whether a bank or one of the company's vendors – have approved your requests for their money and cooperation.

You're not finished yet and there could be surprises in the form of unexpected claims coming into escrow. But the clock is starting to tick down to the day when you'll take over the business, offering up the money and signing the promissory notes as called for in your agreement.

Opening Escrow

The first thing you and the seller will do when opening escrow is to instruct the company about the terms of your deal. As noted earlier, the fee will vary from $1,000 to $10,000 for the basic services. The rate depends on the dollar value of the deal and usually includes the work needed to prepare extra documents and to take care of the filings. Ordinarily the fees are split 50/50 between you and the seller and the escrow firm will probably want some of the money at the beginning. You also will be asked to sign some documents to get things started.

And here are some of the things with which escrow will be involved:

Lien search

A check of the public records is made to determine the rightful owner of the company's equipment and fixtures, and if there are any claims on them. Similar to a title search conducted on real property, this procedure is meant to find out if there are any liens on the personal property used in the business. The search is managed by accessing records for property under the name of the business, or its address or both. It's not unusual to discover that a prior owner or some taxing authority has neglected to remove a lien or claim that has long since been satisfied. And part of the escrow company's job will be to track down the parties and paperwork to verify that the items you are purchasing are free to be sold, just as you were told.

Receiving claims

The escrow holder will hear from anyone who feels they have a claim or interest in the business or any of the property of the business. These will be the responsibility of the seller to handle – either by demonstrating that the claims are not valid or by instructing the escrow holder to pay them. Among the notifications received by escrow, there are likely to be requests from government taxing authorities which enter claims as a matter of course, just to make sure no one is able to close a deal without being current with their obligations.

The escrow officer will review and pass along to the seller any claims that come in. You may or may not be informed about the claims, and since you won't be responsible for them, it isn't critical that you are aware of requests or demands for payment from taxing agencies and others. Many prospective buyers, however, want to be informed about everything having to do with the business they soon expect to own. So you might ask the escrow holder to keep you up to date about the progress of the escrow, the identity of claimants and status of their requests.

Notice of bulk sale and ABC License transfer

The public notice of bulk transfer is conducted for the protection of the buyer (so there will be no claims against the business unknown to you – none of those unpleasant surprises,) and also for the seller's protection (demonstrating that he or she complied with California law and can't be prosecuted by the government or sued by a private party for claims coming out of an improper or illegal transfer.) This notice will be published in a local newspaper that carries legal advertising with you and/or the seller paying another $50 or so for this service. As noted in a previous chapter, once published, you can start the countdown of 12 business days of wait time between the date the notice first appears and the day you can close escrow. This is designed to give any creditors time to notify the escrow – which is named in the notice – that the business owes them money for one reason or another.

And if the business needs a liquor license – either just to sell beer and wine, or approval for full liquor – the escrow will send you and the seller to your local ABC (Alcohol Beverage Control) office to apply for a transfer. There you will obtain a large (about three feet square) notice that is required to be posted to the window of the establishment. And, like the notice of bulk transfer, make sure to have an announcement about the transfer published in an approved paper. This incidentally, applies to cafes that offer beer and wine as well as to restaurants with a full bar, and, of course, grocery and liquor markets. There also is a waiting period associated with this notice, running concurrently with the wait associated with the bulk transfer. But the ABC wait is longer. In many or most cases the ABC Board can spend 60 calendar days or more to complete its investigation of the buyer and the proposed transfer, and in no case does the law permit the license to change hands in fewer than 30 calendar days following posting.

While this is going on, you should check with the planning commission for the town or municipality where the transfer is to take place. It's a good idea to make sure the area is approved for the operation of the business and that the laws are being upheld.

Requesting releases

Even if no taxing authorities have entered a claim, your escrow holder will request clearances from the State Board of Equalization, the IRS, State Franchise Tax Board and the local employment offices just to make sure that the seller is up to date in paying sales taxes, payroll taxes, personal property taxes and so forth.

Verifying approvals

A similar procedure to requesting releases is the escrow's job to contact the landlord to confirm the details you provided about the lease transfer. And, with the landlord's okay, the escrow can help in this action by keeping track of the new lease or lease assignment, getting it signed by the parties and delivering copies at close of escrow. If you will be operating under the seller's current lease, any prorations needed will be handled between you and the seller in escrow. If a new lease is involved, with added payments due to the landlord, escrow may include the landlord in this part of the escrow, having him sign relevant documents and issuing a check for any added rental deposit and/or increased rent.

Approvals needed from institutional or non-institutional lenders also can be verified by the escrow holder. And escrow will make sure any necessary funds to be loaned the buyer are ready when needed, and that loan papers have been properly presented and, at the closing, are signed.

Preparing documents

The loan payments you'll make to the seller will need a promissory note to be official, and that is a document which the escrow ordinarily drafts for both, using standard language, and inserting your name, that of the seller, terms of the loan and a reference to the security agreement, which lists the assets that are used to secure the obligation. Also prepared by escrow can be the other parts of your agreement, such as the covenant not to compete, the training contract and any other deals you and the seller have made to facilitate the transaction.

Waiting it Out

After these tasks are completed, there may be a lull in activity as you wait for expiration of the mandatory periods associated with the published notices. You might want to focus on refining your business plan, setting up accounts with the bank, and the utilities, and filing a fictitious name statement so you'll be able to use the company's trade name. You may want to invite the seller to go with you to the recorder's office in the county where the business is located to sign a release of the name so that you can take it over. This also is a good time to obtain a Federal tax number, which you'll need if you have employees.

And there are a couple of other things you can keep in mind as the clock ticks toward the day when the transfer will be complete. One is to maintain the confidentiality about the impending sale as you promised. It may be hard to keep the secret at this point; a number of people may have been brought in on the situation, such as the landlord, vendors who are planning to work with the buyer for special finance arrangements, and perhaps an employee or two who were taken into the seller's confidence early in the process and sworn to secrecy in return for the promise of an incentive once the deal closes. But I advocate keeping the information as quiet as possible.

I realize that it's hard to keep quiet a fact that has become a matter of public record with publishing in the newspaper. Most of the customers and employees probably are not reading the legal notices, however, and you should make every effort not to talk about the sale, even though, technically, it has been made public.

The other project for this period is to confer with the seller on a training schedule and perhaps plan a little campaign that will go into effect after the close, announcing to customers about your new ownership. This may involve a mailing to everyone on the customer list. Perhaps it will make sense for you and the seller to pay a call on key clients to let them know the news and to make their acquaintance. By planning this out now, you'll be ready to implement the program when the time is right.

The Close

On the day scheduled for close, with the wait time fully elapsed and all needed documents and money in place, the escrow will have a few final important steps to follow to make the transfer official.

You will be asked to bring a certified or cashier's check for the closing amount, which will include the balance of down payment, your share of fees, any deposits to be collected through escrow, any sales or use tax on personal property you've purchased, and the sum of prorated expenses allocated to you.

The rent might be pro-rated so the seller is reimbursed for the part of the month for which you will be the tenant. And the seller probably will get back a lease deposit. These and similar credits to the seller will be handled by escrow and charged to you. Prorations also can apply to rental of equipment, advertising and promotional contracts and other services for which the seller prepaid. Personal property taxes also might be prorated.

After documents are signed and checks distributed – the one for the seller, for the broker if any, for payments to various Federal and State agencies to close the old accounts and to any other entity with a legitimate claim, the escrow will file the documents that need to be publicly recorded. Among them is the security agreement listing personal assets that are being pledged by you as collateral for the loan from the seller. Any other property, including your real estate – if it is being used to secure the obligation – will be identified in an appropriate filing.

This is when the final inventory count is presented to escrow. You will pay the exact amount of money for this, either as part of, or in addition to the price – depending on the agreement.

Once these tasks are completed, the documents signed and notarized, and question are answered, the escrow holder will send you off to celebrate, so he or she can finish with the paperwork.

Conclusion

This review of the final processes is meant to give buyers an idea about the steps that take place once a transaction for sale of a small California business is moved into escrow. There is not much left for the buyer to do except, of course, come up with the money and sign some of the documents needed to finish the deal.

Parties are cautioned that during the waiting period – 12 business days mandatory for a business not needing an ABC license transfer, and at least 30 days, probably 60 days or more, for a business which sells or serves any form of liquor – it's a good idea to talk as little about the sale as possible. And if you're not buying a bar, restaurant or liquor store, you won't be required to post a public notice on the window of the place of business, so it may be possible to keep the secret a little while longer.

Once you've closed – paid the money and signed the documents – you can announce the achievement to whomever you like.

KEY POINTS FROM THIS CHAPTER

❖ *Much of the California law covering the sale and purchase of small businesses is contained in the Uniform Commercial Code, specifying some of the tasks to be completed before a transaction is closed.*

❖ *An escrow will cost from $1,000 to $10,000 based on transaction size, for the basic services. This should include activities such as drafting notes and filing documents.*

❖ *Among the responsibilities of the escrow are to conduct a lien search, assist with the notice of bulk transfer – and in the case of a liquor license transfer – an ABC notice, receive claims, request releases from taxing authorities, verify approvals from lenders and others whose okay is needed to close, prepare documents such as promissory notes, and confer with the parties about claims in the escrow and prorations of rent and other prepaid expenses.*

❖ *There is a mandatory 12 business-day wait for creditors to present claims following publishing of the bulk transfer notice. Escrow can close on the 13th day.*

❖ *The mandatory waiting period in connection with ABC license transfers is a minimum 30 days, from notice publication to closing, but the ABC Board usually requires at least 60 days to conduct its investigation of the buyer and the transfer application.*

❖ *To the extent possible, parties should avoid talking to customers, employees and others about the planned sale. Of course, it'll be hard to keep the secret when the fact of the sale has been published in a legal notice newspaper. And certainly, if an ABC transfer is planned, you can't hide that intent, because the state requires that a big poster be attached to the window of the establishment so it can be read from the outside. Still, the less said, the better. At least until the transfer is completed.*

❖ *The waiting period is a good time to plan the transition and prepare a campaign to announce the change to customers.*

❖ *The landlord for the business may be involved in the escrow if he is to receive additional rent, and/or a new lease is to be signed.*

❖   *Upon closing, the escrow holder will need all the funds scheduled to be distributed to the seller and to any other parties or taxing authorities that have to be paid to clear debts and complete the transaction. Also required will be fees for filings and for any unpaid balance of the escrow fee.*

❖   *Prorations will be calculated and checks distributed by the escrow company, which also is charged with the responsibility of filing any new liens, security agreements and related documents.*

CHAPTER SEVENTEEN

SEEK HELP, ENJOY SUCCESS IN YOUR NEW ROLE

Picture yourself a few weeks after you've taken over as new owner of your business. You're still learning the ropes, meeting the customers, determining if all of the employees are pulling their weight.

Perhaps the income isn't quite what you'd have hoped, but things are improving and as soon as you feel a bit more knowledgeable about everything going on – a little more in control of the business – you plan to begin implementing some of your ideas for improving revenues.

If this is your first business, you undoubtedly are aware of some of the subtle but highly consequential differences represented by your place in the scheme of things, compared to your previous positions as an employee. Among the most profound of these differences, of course, is that when it's your business, you directly benefit from every extra dollar taken in; while every dollar spent – whether wisely or not – comes right out of your pocket. This clearly is one of those circumstances with opportunity mixed in with trouble, and it's up to you to extract the rewards and avoid the opposite.

The same can be said for another profound difference between having a boss and being the boss. When you want things done a certain way it's nice to represent the ultimate authority. What you say is the final word. But what happens when you aren't sure of the best solution for a problem? There's no one higher up to take this responsibility off your shoulders and take the blame should things turn out badly.

Do you miss that cushion? Would it be helpful if you could blame an incompetent supervisor or lazy co-workers for your failure to make the goals you've set out for yourself? Did you appreciate the steady salary you received as someone else's worker, even during those periods when your employer was not making much profit?

Those are some of the luxuries you may have enjoyed as an employee; luxuries you give up in return for the privilege of being your own boss.

It can be lonely at the top, even though your organization may not be very big, and its top is not very high.

But you can take consolation in knowing there are resources available to you.

Go to your local SBA (Small Business Administration) office which most likely will be housed with other federal offices. There you can inquire about SCORE (Service Corps of Retired Executives), a no-charge service that provides counseling to business owners and prospective business owners. The help comes from business executives who donate their time to assist others in reaching success.

This has been a valuable source of support for a number of California business owners. And one good feature is the organization's attempt to match you up with a counselor who is familiar with your business and has valuable, real world experience to offer.

Make sure you get a volunteer with whom you can communicate, and who is genuinely helpful. If your first "counselor" doesn't quite understand what you're trying to accomplish, or whose personality, style or individual characteristics make it difficult to work with him or her, you can request someone with whom you might find it easier to work.

Additionally, you can visit the website, *www.sba.gov.org* which is filled with links to articles, ideas, on-line support and other resources helpful to owners of small businesses. This is a good site to bookmark and refer to from time to time for ideas, or to use as a resource for solving specific problems.

Another option is to enroll in a business course available at one of the California Community College system schools near you. Their business professors can help you to become familiar with the basics of accounting, marketing, management, and other disciplines you feel will help you gain more skills you can apply in your company. A complete list of the more than 100 colleges in the system can be found at *www.ccco.edu*

And if you'd like to get some one-on-one time with a specialist familiar with your business, and you're in a position to pay for the service, there are a number of consultants who might be able to offer just the advice, assistant and encouragement you need to solve problems and move your business forward. Start with your industry's trade group, if there is one. They may be able to refer you to a consultant well versed in your business. Another place to find assistance is to click on the Resources button at *www.bizben.com* and scroll down to the consultants category.

Just as you may have used the help of others – lenders, brokers or agents – to find and acquire the right business, it will be to your advantage to look for, and to call upon resources that will help you make your new enterprise the success you imagined.

For many Americans, the purchase of their own business has led to financial independence and the opportunity to use their skills, their ideas and their energy to mold an enterprise they got from someone else into a completely new business – one which reflects the buyer's creative contribution.

One of the privileges of working as a business broker for a number of years has been my opportunity to witness the transformation of people who may have been mediocre and unsatisfied employees, and suddenly blossomed as creative business entrepreneurs when offered the challenge to run their own enterprise.

This book has been written with the new business buyer in mind. And I wish you the best of luck as you embark on this noble and exciting role as owner of a small California business.

INDEX

Featuring the Successful bizben Method!

NOTES ———————————————————————————————